HERBS
How to Select, Grow and Enjoy

Norma Jean Lathrop

Executive Producer:
  Richard Ray
Contributing Editors:
  Margaret Brandstrom Pavel
  Michael MacCaskey
Photography:
  Michael Landis

Produced by Horticultural Publishing Co., Inc.:
Art Director: Richard Baker
Associate Editors: Lance Walheim and Laura Pick
Research Editor: Dan Burnett; Copy Editor: Bud
Childress; Production Editor: Kathleen Parker;
Design: Judith Hemmerich, Betty Hunter;
Typography: Linda Encinas; Illustration: Roy
Jones; Additional Photography: William Aplin
Cover Photo: Michael Landis

ISBN: 0-89586-077-5
Library of Congress
Catalog Card Number: 80-83064
©1981 HPBooks, Inc.   Printed in U.S.A.
13 12 11 10 9 8

Published by HPBooks
A division of Price Stern Sloan, Inc.
360 N. La Cienega Boulevard
Los Angeles, CA 90048

Herbs: Steeped in Tradition

How would *you* define the term "herb?"

Most of us would probably define it as "something to season food with." But, as a growing body of cooks, gardeners, hobbyists and students of history, geography and nutrition are discovering, there is far more to herbs than that.

"Something to trade with, fight over, import and export"

Historically, herbs and spices are rich in lore and legend, fact and fancy, high romance and good business. You can trace them back through Elizabethan England, ancient Rome and Greece, and through the Bible to the Garden of Eden. You would discover that wars have been fought, trade routes established, lives sold, and cultures, countries and businesses founded— all in the name of the dried, probably ugly, plant parts and the aromatic, flavorful oils they produce.

Geographically, a study of herbs is a look at the world. From our viewpoint in 20th century America, we can easily visualize our forefathers bringing— along with the taste for old country dishes—dill seeds from Scandinavia, sage, oregano and marjoram from the Mediterranean, caraway from Germany, and coriander from the Orient and Mexico. They also brought their faith in the medicinal properties of certain herbs and their pleasure in their aromatic virtues. They brought fennel, chamomile, lavender, yarrow and woodruff. But the new world is only one step in a very long journey. Over the centuries, most herbs have traveled widely. Cumin, for example, came to the United States from Latin America, Germany and Rome, but originated in Egypt. Tarragon came via France from Siberia!

The warm golds of herb-flavored honeys become brilliant when illuminated by the morning sun.

The order and simplicity apparent in the colonial-style home of Mr. and Mrs. Cyrus Hyde of Port Murray, New Jersey, is reflected in the garden of their Well-Sweep Herb Farm, described on page 22. Both house and garden are styled after the tradition of the Shakers, the most notable group of American herbalists.

"Something to heal with . . . and to cast spells with"

As the use of herbs and spices spread throughout the world, beliefs grew in their medicinal and even occult powers. This is not as ridiculous as it may sound. Many of today's medicines are based on chemicals and oils from these plants. Many modern nutritionists emphasize the value of the vitamin and mineral content of herbs.

Few people today would wear an amulet of dill or anise to ward off the evil eye, or tuck cumin into a husband's pocket to keep him from philandering, or use garlic as a charm to attract riches. But many people do chew on cloves to sooth an aching tooth, or apply a paste of mustard to clear a chest cold, or drink a cup of chamomile tea to refresh and soothe. Parsley, for example, is full of vitamins A and C, thiamin, riboflavin, niacin, calcium, iron, magnesium and phosphorous. That makes today's widespread use of parsley as a decorative greenery no more reasonable or scientific than yesterday's belief that using it as a table decoration would ensure mealtime sobriety.

"Something good to smell"

It is not surprising that our frugal, industrious grandparents and great-grandparents valued herbs for their aromatic qualities as much as for their flavor. *Strewing herbs* were spread on floors so they would release their aromas when stepped on. In the last ten years, herbs have become a way to recapture the traditions of our ancestors. Increasing numbers of people are using herbs to make potpourris, sachets, soaps, candles and bath lotions. They are rewarded not only by the product but also by the activities of growing and harvesting the plants, and drying the leaves, seeds and flowers.

But most of all, they are "something to grow"

Depending on our special interest, we can think of herbs as medicines, tonics, nutrients, oils, essences, salves, amulets, love potions, charms, bouquets, sachets, incenses, soaps, shampoos, bath oils, facial and body splashes, seasonings, vinegars, salts, butters, *bouquet garnis*, wines or teas. But primarily, herbs are plants—plants especially suited to home gardens.

Herbs are plants usually grown in temperate climates. Most spices, on the other hand, require a tropical climate. The word "spice" refers to a specific flavor, use or prepared plant part. The word "herb" refers to an entire plant. With few exceptions, spices are not readily grown in home gardens. For this reason only herbs are the dealt with in this book.

The ceiling rafters of the barn at Well-Sweep Herb Farm are covered by a variety of drying herbs and flowers by August. The range of textures and colors is wide and all are natural, no chemicals or dyes are used.

Botanically, an herb is a seed-producing annual, biennial or perennial that does not develop persistent woody tissue. It dies down at the end of a growing season.

The American Herb Society's official definiton is, "Any plant that can be used for pleasure, fragrance or physic." Henry Beston, in *Herbs and the Earth,* says, "An herb is a garden plant which has been cherished for itself and for a use." The Shakers, who did so much in the 18th century to establish interest in herbs in the United States, taught that "Beauty rests on utility. The highest use possesses the greatest beauty." They were probably not thinking of anything as frivolous as the beauty of suburban plots or windowsills. The end products of their acres of basil, borage, horehound, hyssop, marjoram, tansy, sage and thyme were largely medicinal. But their theory of the interdependence of beauty and utility strikes a strong sympathetic note in the hearts of today's home gardeners. Herbs are being grown as ground covers, hedges, borders, rock gardens and container plants.

In the garden, as in the home, it is impossible to think the word "herb" without immediately thinking the word "use." And conversely, for herb enthusiasts, it is just as impossible to think the words "landscape use" without thinking of a specific herb.

Do you need a soft, mowable surface for a children's play area? Plant woolly thyme or chamomile.

Do you need a plant to hold the ground on a sunny slope? Plant a ground-hugging rosemary if climate permits, or perhaps lavender or santolina.

Looking for a plant to creep between stones in a courtyard? Plant creeping thyme or pennyroyal in the sun; Corsican mint in the shade.

Do you want to replace high-maintenance, manicured plants with ones that tend themselves? In the sun try either yarrow or lavender; in the shade consider sweet woodruff.

Do you want a splash of gray for contrast? Consider the artemisias, lavender, santolina or Crete dittany.

True aficionados use herbs in even more specialized ways. They plant herbs to attract bees, discourage pests or to accompany certain vegetables.

Two things make herb gardeners different from other gardeners. The first is their attitude toward the plants they grow. Food gardeners reap. Specialists collect. Home gardeners maintain. Landscape gardeners admire. Herb gardeners become almost personally attached to their plants. You will find—as they have—that thyme or oregano or lavender will give you extra bonuses beyond growth and greenery, and that you are responsible for appreciating, capturing and using

Familiar as a dinner-plate garnish, parsley assumes character and beauty when it flowers in the garden.

all the special gifts they produce. It is easy to feel impersonal about a foundation planting of privet or a bed of petunias. But you cannot avoid getting involved with a chive that suddenly sends forth pretty, dainty, onion-smelling flowers for you to eat. Mint that moves into any available space, swallowing up all plants and weeds in its path.

The second difference involves what you do with your herbs after planting. Herbs generally demand little garden maintenance. The oils that make them flavorful and aromatic also seem to repel pests. But they do demand use. You can start by pinching off the top leaves to flavor a sauce and promote bushiness. Then you might find yourself harvesting, drying and preserving some for winter cooking. Finally you might start distilling and concocting oils for beauty products, producing your own vinegars, teas and dyes. You can press flowers for stationery or make dried arrangements or wreaths for gifts, or use herbs for scenting candles. When you get involved with herbs, one thing leads to another.

In This Book

One of the most popular books in the early days of printing was the *Herbal,* an herb-by-herb rundown of each plant's description and uses. Beginning on page 43 of this book is "A Modern Herbal," a new version of this classic reference. It is devoted particularly to the herbs that do well in the home garden.

"The Modern Herbalists," beginning on page 14, is a visit with outstanding herb gardeners of today and a look at their gardens.

"Herb Gardening," beginning on page 11, tells how to plant, propagate, maintain and harvest herbs. This chapter also includes a listing of nurseries that specialize in herb plants.

"Herbs Are Useful," beginning on page 119, includes tips on using herbs in the kitchen. It also gives directions for making herb vinegars, salts, butters and honeys, herb teas and cosmetics, fragrant potpourri and natural dyes.

The garden and landscape of Norma Jean Lathrop demonstrates the versatility of herbs. This lavender doubles as a low hedge and source of flowers for Norma Jean's lavender sticks, page 149.

The Lathrop Garden

Norma Jean Lathrop is a modern herbalist. Her theme, often repeated in this book, is that *herbs are useful*. Her simple and beautiful garden contains plants that she uses in a virtually infinite number of ways, from teas to medicines to paper making.

What kind of person is a modern herbalist?

"I grew up just 12 miles from the Mexican border in California's Imperial Valley. Among my earliest memories are the wonderful smells of rich and spicy Mexican cooking.

"The Imperial Valley is, of course, a rich agricultural area. Living there, you are surrounded by growing plants. Most people living there were commercial farmers, as were my grandparents.

"My father always had an outstanding vegetable garden. He grew picture-perfect vegetables of all kinds. My mother was just as successful in her flower garden. She grew many flowering herbs. Some of her favorites

were calendula, larkspur, foxglove, nasturiums and poppies.

"My curiosity in herbs began when I was a young girl. While reading the Bible I noticed the many references to herbs. Later while raising our family I became interested in herbs and nutrition.

"Years later, in 1971, I first heard about a local unit of the Herb Society. I had some extra time, was as curious as before, so I decided to attend a meeting. I met some wonderful people at that first meeting. They were so knowledgeable and eager to share their experience that it seemed a pleasure just to be around them.

"Then I took some classes at the Los Angeles State and County Arboretum, and after that, I did some teaching of my own. I volunteered to talk about herbs with elementary schoolchildren, and to make displays for the Arboretum on various aspects of herbalism. Each display was meticulously researched. They were a marvelous learning experience and the way I really began to learn about herbs.

"Naturally my own garden began to grow. We didn't approach it with an overall plan. Friends would give me plants, I'd bring them home and try to find room for them.

"Our climate here is very mild. Our half-acre is in the foothills and was formerly an avocado orchard. Our only garden space was a horrible, weedy, rocky hill in the back yard.

"The soil is mostly decomposed granite, so it was difficult to get some plants to grow. I wish now we had been able to add more organic matter to improve the soil. But on the other hand, the soil drains very quickly. Most herbs do well, once established, even in poor soil. Of course we had to build terraces. The slope was so steep it was hard to keep your footing. Some of the original terraces have evolved into the raised beds you can see today.

Norma Jean is harvesting thyme, which is used for cooking, potpourris, herb baths and cosmetics.

The side garden has a fragrant border of sweet marjoram.

Left: In the Lathrop garden: **1.** Trailing rosemary **2.** Lavender **3.** Scented geranium **4.** Upright rosemary **5.** Fig **6.** Wisteria **7.** Rose.

"When friends ask me to help them plan an herb garden, my first question is 'What kind of plants do you want?' I tell them that is where it must start. Most want a kitchen garden, but some are interested in medicinal herbs, dyeing herbs or others. Once I know their interest, I recommend sources so they can read about them. After that it's no more than common sense.

"I think most herb gardens—mine is, for sure—are really a collection of several different kinds of gardens. For instance, I've grouped most of my favorite tea plants—black stem peppermint, lemon verbena and lemongrass—into one bed. In another area are my favorite potpourri plants—'Dainty Bess' roses, orris and vetiver root. Naturally I have a bed of kitchen herbs—rosemary, lemon thyme, marjoram, bay, winter savory and coriander.

"The one idea I'd really like to get across is that herbs are *useful*. I'm still amazed by how much my own herb garden contributes to me and my family."

Herb Gardening

Herbs are easy to grow. The essential oils that produce flavor and fragrance occur in greatest quantities and concentration when herbs receive at least six hours of sunshine a day and are growing in soil that is not too rich. Except for a few such as angelica, sweet cicely and sweet woodruff, which prefer partial shade, most herbs do best in a sunny location.

HERBS IN THE LANDSCAPE

Throughout history, mankind's search for beauty has included an esteem for herbs. At one extreme, people planted herbs in formal gardens in which the beds and paths were carefully measured and precisely maintained. Others let herbs run rampant in luxuriant, tangled abandon. Either way, herbs were grown for harvest, but people could enjoy their contribution to the landscape as well.

LANDSCAPE PLANNING WITH HERBS

Today, we still plant our favorite herbs for use in teas, potpourris, medicine chests or stews, but we can admire them, too, as they grow in our gardens. Herbs can add many elements to a landscape. Here are some suggestions.

Texture—Some herbs are fine, dainty and lacy: Sweet cicely, parsley, coriander, fennel, winter savory, thyme, lady's bedstraw, yarrow and southernwood are a few.

Some are tropical and verdant: Horseradish, nasturtium, comfrey, betony and lady's mantle are examples.

Color—Most herbs are bright and light green like basil, parsley, spearmint and violets. Some are dark and deep, like thyme and chives, or shadowed like rosemary and tarragon. There is a purple basil and a number of herbs with golden, variegated leaves.

But some—santolina, southernwood, wormwood and lavender—are various shades of gray: ghostly, wispy and light-reflecting. These are widely used by

Choose plants for your herb garden to suit your taste, but don't feel restricted to using only herbs. Betty Stevens uses yellow daylilies, front and left, to brighten her herb garden. There is more about her garden on page 30.

Smaller beds help contain spreading herbs, such as mint or tarragon, and pathways make frequent harvesting easier.

best planted where you can touch it to get the fragrance. Angelica and lovage, lemon verbena and anise will easily reach higher than 4 feet. Sweet bay, if allowed, can become a 50-foot tree.

Sweet woodruff is a wonderful carpeting herb. It grows 2 to 5 inches high and takes shade and dry soil. It can be mowed and accepts a footstep now and then. It is the unique, memorable flavoring of May wine—see page 140.

Woolly thyme is another excellent ground cover. It is low growing, 2 to 3 inches high, and has an endearing way of creeping into crevices and spilling over walls. You might want to blend several thymes: woolly, mother-of-thyme, white creeping and pink creeping thyme. The shades and hues of their pastel flowers make a beautiful blend.

Mass—Rosemary is a plant without peer wherever it is hardy. Tall-growing forms are breathtaking against rocks, fences and in large containers. Prostrate forms are intriguing in tubs, hanging baskets, atop low walls or anywhere they can flow downward like slow-motion water.

Habit—Beware of the mints. As lovable as they are, they are also invasive. They often strangle other herbs in the same bed. Plant them in a separate bed or control their spread by planting in sunken pots, flue tiles or any similar confining material. Mints also cross-pollinate. To maintain the individual qualities of spearmint, peppermint or applemint, plant them in separate beds. Once their flowers and roots have mingled, you'll have a tough time distinguishing one from another.

French tarragon is another spreader that can take over smaller herbs and herb beds. Tarragon and mint are two good reasons many herb gardens are carefully divided into many separate beds.

PLAN AHEAD

Establishing an herb garden, large or small, deserves a bit of forethought. Even without advance planning, you will probably succeed. Herbs are persistent, beautiful, almost disease-free and have a way of establishing themselves, once planted. But you will do even better, and will probably appreciate your garden more, if you take a bit of time to plan ahead.

These are some of the points to bear in mind:

What does each plant need? Does it need sun or shade, clay or sandy soil, water or drought? Meet these needs and the plant will reward you twelvefold.

Never be fooled by its size in the pot you buy. You are buying a baby with surprising potential. Give your plant room not only for reaching and spreading, but also for self-sowing.

landscape architects. If you are creating your own design, don't overlook this end of the spectrum. The soothing, receding tones of an all-gray corner or far-wall patch become eerily bright on a moonlit night, and will reflect available light in surprising ways throughout the day.

Don't neglect flower color. Herbs that do have bright and showy flowers accent and enliven the garden. For instance, dyer's chamomile adds a generous amount of mustard yellow to the garden from midsummer on. Yellow, flat-topped yarrow flowers are among the longest lasting. The scarlet flowers of bee balm, *Monarda didyma,* complement the more subdued lavender, and contrast with the bright yellow of tansy.

Form—Herbs may be small and dainty, gentle and feathery, or big and rambunctious. Diminutive Corsican mint usually grows no higher than 1/2 inch and is

The most cold-sensitive herbs, such as lemon verbena, rosemary and bay, can be grown in any climate if sheltered during winter. These bay laurel trees are in a Michigan garden.

How much do you value convenience? Plant your herbs near the kitchen door if that spot is likely to suit it. Make the location convenient to paths or stepping stones.

Soil and fertilizer—Any good garden soil will support a productive herb garden. A soil pH of neutral to slightly alkaline is best. Amend acid soil with lime. Good drainage is essential. Improve poorly drained sites by deep cultivation or by adding organic matter. Raised beds are the best answer to problems caused by slow drainage.

Once established, most herbs prefer a rather dry soil and require water only during long droughts. Exceptions are herbs such as mint, angelica and lovage, which require moist soil.

If you want your herb garden to be attractive as well as productive, pay attention to soil preparation and periodic fertilization. Prepare the soil as you would for a vegetable or flower garden. This means opening and cultivating the soil, breaking up the larger clods and

adding organic matter. Manures and composts dissipate quickly and their effects are short-lived. If your soil is decomposed granite or similarly thin or compact, choose a long-lasting organic material such as a wood by-product. These prevent compaction, allow air circulation in heavy soils and help retain moisture and nutrients in thin, grainy soils. Most last up to three years. By that time your herb garden will be well established and self-supporting.

In good soils, additional fertilizer might not be necessary. Fertilizer will increase growth but not the production of essential oils. In rich soils herb plants will be more attractive, but weak in flavor and fragrance.

Most herb gardeners who fertilize on a regular basis use a well-rotted manure, cottonseed meal or similar organic-based fertilizer. Almost any kind of fertilizer will work as well if you follow package directions.

Keep established plantings free of weeds with regular cultivation or use a mulch. Wood chips, shredded bark, buckwheat hulls or similar materials significantly reduce weed growth and prevent soil from splashing onto plants during watering.

Pests—Herbs are relatively free from pests. But problems do occasionally appear.

Root rot is sometimes troublesome with woody, perennial herbs, especially the ones native to rocky Mediterranean slopes. Their roots and stems have never developed resistance to excessive water. If your soil drains poorly, you can either add long-lasting organic matter to the soil so that air can circulate more easily, or you can plant in raised beds or mounds, which automatically create excellent drainage.

Whiteflies and aphids are indiscriminate feeders and might attack certain herb plants, especially in spring. Various sprays help contain the spread of these pests, notably diazinon, malathion, pyrethrum and synthetic pyrethrum derivatives. Or you can simply wash pests away with a strong stream of water or a spray of 1 tablespoon detergent per gallon of water. If you use soapy water, wash the plant with fresh water a day or two later to prevent the soap from damaging the leaves.

Rust eventually appears on mints in most gardens, and sometimes on violets. Sprays, such as copper sulfate, will limit this fungus, but mint is so prolific it's not reasonable to worry too much about it. The disease does not affect underground stems and runners, so one way to eliminate it is to remove and burn all the stems above ground. Or move some roots to another spot and start a new plant.

Modern Herbalists

At one time, there was no distinction between an herbalist and a botanist. An herbalist was a person who knew about all plants and their uses. Today, scientific botany has grown to the point where most botanists are specialists, so the meaning of the term "herbalist" has changed. Now herbalists are people who specialize in useful plants.

The following pages are devoted to the words of some of today's best herb gardeners, along with photographs of their gardens.

You will find formal and informal gardens. Many incorporate designs commonly called a *knot* garden. This is an English term for garden design based on patterns used by weavers and lace makers and popular from the 16th century to late 18th century. This type of garden has become popular with many modern herbalists.

The advice of these herbalists is practical and their gardens are inspiring. You'll also find that their enthusiasm is catching!

Growing interest in herbs is indicated by the expanding membership of the Herb Society of America and its frequent and lively meetings. This group is touring the herb garden at the Los Angeles State and County Arboretum.

Herbs are an important part of the landscape around the home of Nancy and Stephen Hamilton of St. Helena, California.

Herb Selection Guide

Annual herbs
Anise
Basil
Borage
Chamomile, German
Chervil
Coriander
Cumin
Dill
Fennel
Marigold, pot
Marjoram, sweet
Savory, summer

Perennial herbs
Angelica
Agrimony
Artemisia
Bergamot
Catnip
Chamomile, Roman
Chives
Comfrey
Costmary
Fennel
Feverfew
Germander
Horehound
Hyssop
Lavender
Lemon balm
Lovage
Marjoram
Mints
Mugwort
Oregano
Rosemary
Rue
Sage

Savory, winter
Sorrel
Southernwood
Sweet cicely
Tansy
Tarragon
Thyme
Wormwood
Yarrow

Biennial herbs
Borage
Caraway
Chervil
Parsley
Sage, clary

Attractive flowers
Bee balm
Borage
Carnation
Feverfew
Foxglove
Iris
Nasturtium
Soapwort
Yarrow

Gray garden
Crete dittany
Germander
Germander, shrub
Horehound
Lamb's-ears
Lavender
Lavender cotton
Licorice
Mugwort
Rue
Sage
Santolina

Society garlic
Southernwood
Thyme, 'Silver Posie'
Thyme, woolly
Yarrow, woolly
Wormwood

Tolerate shade
Angelica
Chervil
Comfrey
Costmary
Lemon balm
Mints (except catnip)
Parsley
Pennyroyal
Sweet cicely
Sweet woodruff
Tarragon, French
Thyme, lemon

Evergreen perennials
Burnet, salad
Germander
Horehound
Hyssop
Lavender
Marjoram, winter
Rue
Sage
Santolina
Savory, winter
Southernwood
Thyme, common

Backgrounds
Angelica
Bay laurel
Fennel
Hollyhock
Lovage

Sage, clary
Sunflower

Hedges
Basil, tree
Lavender
Rosemary
Sage
Santolina
Southernwood
Wormwood

Low borders
Artemisia 'Silver Mound'
Boxwood
Catnip
Chives
English ivy
Garlic, society
Germander
Hyssop
Parsley
Santolina
Thyme, common
Savory, winter

Ground covers
Catnip
Chamomile, Roman
Germander, dwarf
Lamb's-ears
Lavender cotton
Lavender, English
Mint, corsican
Rosemary, prostrate
Sweet woodruff
Thyme, woolly
Yarrow

Tolerate moist soil
Angelica
Bergamot
Comfrey
Lady's mantle
Lovage
Mints (except catnip)
Parsley
Pennyroyal
Sweet flag
Valerian
Violets

Tolerate dry soil
Borage
Burnet
Chamomile
Chives
Crete dittany
Fennel
Feverfew
Geranium
Germander
Lady's bedstraw
Lavender
Pennyroyal

Rosemary
Sage
Santolina
Savory
Soapwort
Southernwood
Thyme
Wormwood
Yarrow

Marjoram

Attract bees
Basil
Borage
Catnip
Chamomile
Fennel
Germander
Hyssop
Lavender
Lemon balm
Marjoram
Rosemary
Sage
Savory, winter
Sweet cicely

Attract hummingbirds
Campanula
Catnip
Foxglove
Larkspur
Sage, Mexican
Monarda
Pineapple sage
Salvia
Soapwort

Germander

Herbs For A Hillside

Clara Rygiol of Diamond Bar, California, has a family heritage that is tightly linked to herbs. With her wonderful eastern European accent, which seemed to bring us closer to her past, she told of her experiences with herbs:

"I have been growing herbs all my life. My father was very interested in growing herbs for his bees in Poland and my mother used them for culinary purposes. Herbs were all around me as I grew up.

Distinctions between functional landscape plants, kitchen herbs and flowering perennials are lost in the hillside garden of Clara Rygiol. Here she strolls through a ground cover of gazanias bordered by the gray foliage of *Artemisia arborescens.*

"When I was young, I was considered an herb doctor. It was very mild medicine, but I would use garden herbs and some wild varieties to treat mild illnesses.

"I've only had my present herb garden for two years. The hillside was nothing but weeds. We cleared it, then each day I would spend a few hours planting herbs. It took a long time. Now I have over 200 types planted. We use Rainbird overhead sprinklers and Osmocote slow-release fertilizer scattered around the herbs and container plants.

"Fragrant and culinary herbs are my favorite. I'm a continental cook so I always need herbs. I smoke turkey, chicken, fish and cornish hens, but first I marinate them in herbs—bay leaves, thyme, marjoram, basil—with some vinegar and a little salt. I have a special herb blend with 12 different herbs in exact proportions. You would be surprised how much better it makes everything taste, compared to a briné marinade.

"I also make rose petal jam from fragrant hybrid tea roses. 'Chrysler Imperial' is my favorite. My candied angelica is considered the best.

"I use the old-fashioned method to store my herbs—I pack them in salt in a jar and keep them in the refrigerator. First I put in a layer of herbs, then some kosher salt, then more herbs and so on, see page 122 for instructions. It works very well. You can just pull out a branch or two as you need for sauce or soup. And it works with any type of herb. I dry herbs for my herb blends."

1. Society garlic **2.** St. John's wort **3.** Agrimony **4.** Rue **5.** Lemon balm **6.** Foxglove **7.** Row of English lavenders **8.** Rosemary **9.** Costmary **10.** Mullein **11.** Geranium **12.** Artemisia **13.** Coreopsis **14.** Nutmeg geranium **15.** Lime **16.** Blue sage **17.** Rose geranium.

Cranbrook House Garden

Cranbrook House Gardens in Bloomfield Hills, Michigan, was started by Mr. and Mrs. George C. Booth in 1908. It is famous locally for its continuous bloom of trees, shrubs, bulbs, annuals and perennials. In 1971, an equally spectacular herb garden was added to the grounds by the Southern Michigan Unit of The American Herb Society. Society volunteers still tend the garden. We spoke with a very active member, Carolyn Jamison:

"A group of us got together and planned the garden. There are three beds. Two are 10 by 10 feet and the other is 10 by 17 with two 4 by 40-foot strips along its sides. There is no definite theme, but we did try to stay with an Old English style, which complements the house. Most of the plants are perennial so we don't have to dig them up every winter. However, there are a few things we protect such as a big bay tree in a container that is kept in a garage all winter. Some tender perennial herbs, such as French tarragon, rosemary and lemon verbena, are treated as annuals.

"We garden organically, adding compost and manure to the soil and usually a little bonemeal in spring. It takes a few hours to get the garden in shape in spring and then again in fall, but otherwise it requires about an hour a week. That adds up to about 40 hours over a season.

"The herbs that are harvested and used in potpourris and wreaths are sold at either the Cranbrook plant sale in fall or the Herb Society sale."

1. Artemisia 'Silver King' **2.** Germander **3.** Purple sage **4.** Red creeping thyme **5.** Catnip **6.** Boxwood **7.** Lamb's-ears **8.** Giant onion **9.** Common thyme **10.** Tansy **11.** Lavender **12.** Rose.

Formal Home Garden

Phyllis and Frederick Boss of Manchester, Connecticut, have many garden interests, including herbs. They moved into their present home more than 25 years ago. Their plant knowledge and design flair are evident in the beautiful formal garden pictured on these pages. Phyllis tells the story:

"We bought the house in 1954 and began gardening then. It had been empty for ten years, and it was pretty wild. My husband was interested in formal gardens, and raising boxwoods was his hobby. He started with only one plant and now we have more than a thousand.

"So we started with a boxwood garden and gradually added perennials, herbs and annuals. I have a special section where I keep the kitchen herbs, and I try to keep the gray plants together, but otherwise I just spread the herbs around.

"My favorite herbs for the kitchen are thyme, sage, marjoram, basil and parsley. I don't use too many exotic things. I dry and freeze some herbs. I also make potpourris with lemon balm and pineapple sage. I save all the petals from the fragrant flowers too. We keep a lot of flowers in the garden—zinnias, marigolds, petunias—especially things we can cut and bring inside. Our garden is very colorful.

"Japanese beetle is our worst pest and all we can really do against them is try to trap them. But if the whole neighborhood doesn't fight them, it is hard to keep them under control.

"We use a mulch in winter to protect the plants after the ground has frozen. I dig up some of the tender ones and bring them inside. The room isn't very warm. We keep it anywhere from 40° to 60° F (5° to 15° C). The herbs don't grow much. We just keep them alive so we can make cuttings to plant next spring."

The Boss herb garden is informal enough to be located in the back yard of a modern home. With the border of boxwood, it becomes traditionally formal, too.

Here is the herb garden formula that has been good for centuries: lots of color and texture, and a boxwood hedge to hold it together.

Right: **1.** Boxwood **2.** Pink yarrow **3.** Gold yarrow **4.** Scented geranium **5.** Zinnia **6.** Larkspur **7.** Mugo pine **8.** Chives **9.** Cardamom **10.** Lady's mantle **11.** Sweet cicely **12.** Chrysanthemum **13.** Sweet alyssum **14.** Germander

The Cloisters—History and Tradition

The Cloister herb garden is modeled in both design and plants on a 12th Century herb garden. Its similarity to modern gardens demonstrates the continuity of the herb garden idea.

The Cloisters, a branch of The New York Metropolitan Museum of Art, is a museum of medieval art situated in Fort Tryon Park overlooking the Hudson River. The park, the building and most of the collections were made available to the public with the financial backing of John D. Rockefeller, Jr. Opened in 1938, this modern structure in medieval style incorporates sections from such monuments as a 12th century chapter house, parts of cloisters from five medieval monasteries, a Romanesque chapel and a 12th century Spanish apse.

In the center of The Cloisters is a very special herb garden. Susan Leach, head gardener and historical botanist, describes it:

"The herb garden is actually one of the collections of The Cloisters and is built on the theme of a monastery. The word *cloisters* means enclosure. Architecturally, it is a series of columns around an open area exposed to the sky with a pretty little walkway inside the columns. In an actual monastery it would have been the center of all activity. The garden itself is a composite of medieval garden structures and plant materials. This includes raised beds, wattle fences woven from osier twigs, plants in containers and topiary plants. Herb gardens were essentially utilitarian, with plants chosen for their medicinal and culinary qualities. Traditionally, too, the plant material was relatively delicate and could be grown in small places. Larger crops and fruit trees were grown outside the walls.

"There are roughly 220 plants in the herb garden. Some have uses dating back to before 1520. This is something we are very precise about. We do a lot of research looking for medieval references to the use of a particular herb before we plant it here. Part of my job is to look around The Cloisters and see which plant materials are represented in tapestries and paintings and then to display them properly in the garden.

"We do have some old herbals that we use. We rely heavily on a list of plants that Charlemagne wanted grown in the Imperial Gardens of Iceen. I believe there are about 75 plants mentioned.

"Not all the herbs grown here are culinary. We have divided them up into plants that are aromatic, those that would have been medicinal, dye plants, vegetable seasoning, salad type herbs and salad spices.

"Besides organizing plants according to use, we pay very close attention to physical requirements as well. Of course, we make sure that the shade-loving plants are situated under trees, and those that like full sun are against bright walls. But we also group some of the tender plants—such as French lavender, thyme and dittany—so they can be protected by a portable cold frame in winter.

"We use a buckwheat mulch to keep the soil from drying out rapidly. It is an attractive mulch and a nice way to display the plants. We also have a regular program of clipping and trimming the herbs. Each herb is trimmed according to how it is to be used. People expect to see the flowers on lavender or leafy foliage of basil. This takes a lot of time but we have a nicer garden for it.

"We use the herbs as much as we can around the museum. I always try to keep a big herb bouquet in the front hall and usually decorate parts of the museum around Christmas. I like to feel that both the plants and the museum benefit from my trimming."

Right: **1.** Quince **2.** Honeysuckle **3.** Mullein **4.** Pot marigold **5.** Garden sorrell **6.** Wall valerian **7.** Rampion **8.** Elecampane **9.** Horseradish **10.** Leeks **11.** French sorrel **12.** Good King Henry **13.** Skirret **14.** Tansy.

Well-Sweep Herb Farm

Well-Sweep Herb Farm takes its name from this monument to the simple life—a 19th century well-sweep.

Well-Sweep Herb Farm, Port Murray, New Jersey, is a marvelous source of common and unusual herb plants, and a very special place to visit. The garden and nursery are designed and maintained by Mr. and Mrs. Cyrus Hyde. Mr. Hyde tells of their special relationship with herbs:

"Herbs are in our blood. I was born and raised in a house that was in our family for more than 200 years. We always had a garden. We raised our own food, or at least a good part of it. We had a root cellar under our barn where we would store potatoes, apples, carrots and things like that all winter long.

"As a kid I would hang this or that in our wagon-house where we had all sorts of thing drying. As I grew up, I forgot about most of these things. But after I was married I started a small herb garden for my wife and we began drying herbs again. I started to sell a few things to people with colonial kitchens and before I knew it, my hobby had snowballed into a business. My wife happens to be a very good cook, which makes raising herbs even more interesting. She also makes wreaths out of dried flowers that we sell all over the country.

"We have lived in our present house for 14 years and I started the garden a year after we moved in. It wasn't easy. Although it is a small piece of property, about 4-1/4 acres, the soil was poor and rocky and the land was covered with trees. We had to clear the land and build up the soil.

"As for the garden itself, I believe an herb garden should reflect the owner. For instance, if I design an herb garden for someone, I try to take something from that person or the place they live in and use it in the design. If it is a big English manor, I might use a traditional knot garden for the center and plant herbs all around it.

"Personally, I love formal gardens and I am a collector, so I have laid out our garden in a formal manner to display my collection. I have 80 types of scented geraniums planted in beds with 30 or more different lavenders. I don't even know how many basils I have. Most herb farms will have two or three types of rosemary. I have at least 24.

"I've been collecting for quite a few years and have many unusual varieties. I've set up an educational herb garden that people come to see from all over the world. It is a look-and-learn garden. And we sell herbs, too.

"When it comes to the actual growing of the herbs, I'm strictly an organic farmer. We believe as the Bible says, 'Give and you shall receive.' If you expect the plants to grow, you're going to have to put something in the soil every year. So it is a continuous process of adding horse, cow or chicken manure, or whatever we have, to the soil each year.

"At Well-Sweep we have never destroyed nature's balance in our garden, so on the whole we are not bothered by many insects. You see, when you spray you kill the good insects as well as the bad. This often

Right: Cyrus Hyde shown in his garden. **1.** Tricolor sage **2.** Common sage **3.** Thyme **4.** Gray santolina **5.** Germander **6.** Creeping white thyme **7.** Rosemary **8.** Oregano **9.** Basil **10.** German chamomile. To the left is Roman chamomile. **11.** Lemon verbena **12.** Pineapple sage **13.** Allium **14.** Savory **15.** Santolina **16.** Nepeta **17.** Rue **18.** Poppy **19.** Myrtle.

The path to the storage room is lined with lamb's-ears and an occasional poppy.

creates a vacuum that favors the troublemakers. Then you are worse off than when you started, or at least you are committed to more spraying.

"We don't have to water often. Our soil is on the clay side, but we have added a lot of organic material so it holds moisture well. We also use a shredded licorice root mulch that is very good at holding moisture. We don't dig it right into the soil because as it breaks down it takes away nitrogen. We remove the mulch every year, put it on the compost pile to break down, then add it to the soil the next year as compost.

"Our winters in New Jersey's northwest are too cold for many of our tender herbs, so I dig them up and overwinter them in a cold frame or in one of our two greenhouses. The main secret to doing this is to dig up the plants early enough so they can be kept outside to recover before being brought inside. Otherwise, you're stepping on them twice. Cutting the roots and then moving the plants into dry indoor conditions is a double shock. Dig them up, let them develop new roots, *then* bring them indoors."

Right: **1.** Dwarf crimson pigmy barberry **2.** Dwarf hyssop **3.** Lavender **4.** Lemon verbena trained as a standard **5.** Rosemary trained as a standard **6.** Germander **7.** Dwarf pomegranate **8.** Licorice verbena **9.** Miniature geranium **10.** Scented geraniums **11.** Damask rose 'Belladonna'.

These trees are actually rosemary which Cyrus has trained as a standard over the last several years. The low hedge that borders and crosses the bed is germander. The mulch is shredded licorice root.

Caprilands Herb Farm

Caprilands Herb Farm is located in North Coventry, Connecticut. It is the creation of Adelma Simmons and it is best described in her own words:

"I've lived in this 18th century house since 1929. I didn't really develop an herb garden until I retired, which is funny because I used to work 18 hours a day. Now it seems I work 24 hours a day. We have 50 acres of land and have developed 8 acres. The rest is pasture and woodland.

"The herb garden started in 1935 when I planted a dooryard garden close to the house. Then I had no thought of inviting the public, but a few friends would come over, and then garden clubs visited. Now we have a full program for visitors.

"Our day usually starts with a lecture in the barn. Popular subjects include herbs for flavor, for fragrance and for fun; planning and planting the herb garden; and plans and plants for the gray garden. The topics vary with the season.

"After the lecture there is a tour of the farm. We visit the 30 or so individual gardens or plantings. Each has its own theme: the gray or silver garden, the Victorian garden, the Shakespeare garden, the dye garden and so on. We have a summer staff of about 18 that cares for the gardens and answers questions.

"The tour is followed by a luncheon. The aim of the luncheon is to allow visitors to experience the greatest number of herb tastes we can provide, and then give information about each one. The meal will include a main dish cooked with herbs, homemade bread, herb jellies, teas and punch.

"Everything on the farm is for sale. There are plants, seeds, books, dried herbs, and of course, live plants. In the front rooms of the house we have handmade dolls, sachets, scented pillows, herb and flower wreaths, spice bags, potpourris and pomanders.

1. Germander **2.** Catnip **3.** Blue spirea **4.** Michaelmas daisies **5.** Golden thyme **6.** Silver mound artemisia **7.** Lemon verbena **8.** Rosemary **9.** Goutweed **10.** Atlas cedar **11.** Pink yarrow **12.** Pot marigold **13.** Black-eyed Susan **14.** Ajuga **15.** Silver oats **16.** Variegated dogwood.

The Capriland gray garden is a feast for the eye, a switch from the usual greens or bright colors. It begins in the center with a statue of Pan surrounded by lamb's-ears and santolina. At the left is blue-flowering lavender, at the rear is an olive tree and at the right is artemisia. A grass, silver oats, is in the foreground.

"One of my enthusiasms is the study of legends and farming festivals, and many of the festivals are celebrated regularly at Caprilands: the summer solstice, Michaelmas, All Saints' Day, Advent and, of course, Christmas.

"Caprilands is the realization of my dream. It meant the rehabilitation of a very old, worn-out farm and neglected land. Once it was a trash heap. Now it has been transformed into a thing of beauty: our herb garden."

Saint Fiacre, the gardener's patron saint, presides over a bed of germander and santolina.

Circular Herb Garden

The herb garden of Paula Fishman and Louis Savette of Santa Monica, California, turned out to be more than just a hobby. It developed into a profitable business. Paula tells how it got started:

"The house we're in now is new to me. I started growing herbs at my old house, and going into business was little more than a fluke. I joined the local Herb Society and they have a recipe in one of their cookbooks called Best Salad Vinegar. I started making it and passing it out to my friends. Before I knew it I had a little business.

"Now I make four kinds of vinegars. Two are based on red wine: 'Italian Garden' made from oregano, bay and garlic, and 'Lusty' with *lots* of garlic and rosemary. The 'Best Salad' vinegar is made from cider vinegar with dill, mint and garlic. I also make a white wine vinegar with shallots and tarragon. It is called 'Perfect.'

"I started out growing all the herbs I needed, but the demand for my vinegars has reached the point where I have to buy several herbs. The back of the house is designed like an Old English country garden with lots of flowers. The herbs grow in circular raised beds made of cement. There are also some broken concrete raised beds, which is a nice way to recycle old concrete.

"The front of the house is planted with silver and gray herbs—things like creeping thyme, rosemary, eucalyptus and santolina. It is very handsome."

The Fishman-Savett garden uses concrete raised beds to grow many herbs. In the front bed, a square of lemon thyme is surrounded by gray, old-woman wormwood and dwarf sage. In the rear bed, clockwise from top, are parsley, oregano, sorrel and marjoram. Also shown are lemon verbena, lemon balm and scented geranium.

Large, concrete raised planters are an interesting variation of traditional herb garden design.

Right: **1.** Daylily **2.** Society garlic **3.** Spearmint **4.** Sorrel **5.** Yarrow **6.** Sea lavender **7.** Ranunculus **8.** Marguerite **9.** Parsley **10.** Oregano **11.** Lavender **12.** Chervil **13.** Snow-in-summer.

Triangular Herb Garden

The home of Robert and Betty Stevens of Cobalt, Connecticut, dates back to 1806. Rather than renovate an old lawn behind their home, they decided to put in an herb garden.

An herb garden must have an idea or plan. Theirs was to organize it according to how the herbs were to be used. They divided their 40 by 40-foot plot into four equal triangles separated by walkways. One triangle was planted with herbs that attract bees, another

The gardens shown clockwise from 12 o'clock are the bee garden, fragrance garden, culinary garden and decorative garden. See text for herbs used in each garden.

with culinary herbs, the third with decorative herbs and the last with fragrant herbs. Betty Stevens talks about her four herb gardens:

"I use herbs all the time. It is like eating peanuts—once you start you can't stop. For instance, when we moved into this old house, which has a dirt cellar, I soon found that I would have to do something to combat the musty odor. You know—that old house smell. So I started growing herbs that I could bring into the house to freshen up the air.

"Southernwood, which is planted in the fragrant garden and throughout all the other gardens, is used fresh-cut during summer. I put it under rugs, sofa and chair cushions, and mattresses to freshen the rooms during the humid weather. I then dry the southernwood and use it in a moth-repellent mixture with tansy, santolina, wormwood, cloves and crushed cinnamon sticks. Bags of this mixture go into closets and storage chests.

"Most of the leaves and flowers of the plants in the fragrant garden are mixed with petals from the old rose species, *Rosa gallica,* to make potpourri. I also add colorful petals from the flowers that are growing in the vegetable garden, such as larkspur, marigold, Johnny-jump-ups, feverfew or other roses.

"Although I do not raise bees, a neighbor of ours does and he often shares his honey. I use the bee herbs in other ways, but always leave plenty of blossoms for the bees. See page 15 for herbs to attract bees.

"From the culinary garden, I dry savory, tarragon, oregano, marjoram, sage and rosemary. I chop and freeze dill, parsley, chives, basil, lovage and a mixture of everything. I also make herb butter with tarragon, basil, savory and rosemary, and freeze it. I make vinegar from basil, dill and tarragon.

"The decorative herbs are used in Williamsburg or colonial-style dried arrangements, herb wreaths and beam bundles, colorful bunches of herbs to hang from beams in the house. During the summer they are used in fresh bouquets. Anything left over ends up in potpourris.

"In my opinion, preparing for winter is the hardest part about growing my herbs. I just don't like to garden when its cold. First I cut everything back and clean up the dead leaves that have dropped from the maple trees. They don't make a good mulch because they mat. Instead, we lay down evergreen bows after the ground has completely frozen.

"I bring tender herbs, such as rosemary and lemon verbena, indoors gradually. First I root prune, then after they've had a chance to develop new feeder roots, I take them out of the ground and bring them to the back porch. Finally, I move them to the basement under artificial light. I reverse the process in spring."

Herbs and Roses

Mrs. Margaret O'Neill of San Marino, California, inherited her interest in herbs from her English mother:

"I guess because of her, I've always been interested in English history. When we were in Europe, I went through quite a few of the gardens and picked up some English garden books. So many of the gardens there have herbs in them, it seemed only natural to want to grow them.

"When I started growing herbs I was restricted to small pots on my patio because of lack of space. I concentrated on the culinary herbs. My favorites are marjoram, summer savory and thyme. They are part of the ancient French mixture called *fines herbes*. Because I cook mainly vegetables, stews, soups and such, they go in almost everything.

"Soon I just had to have more garden space. So we enclosed part of our front yard with a circular wall about 3 feet high. In the English manner, the main circle is my rose garden, backed by a privet hedge. In front are small beds of herbs. The design is based on the old monastery gardens of England, where they walled the gardens to protect them from the wind.

"I began by planting the strongly fragrant *strewing herbs* that come from the days of earthen floors when things weren't so sanitary. People would throw rushes, a grass-like plant, on the ground to walk on. Among the rushes they would strew the strongly fragrant herbs, such as thyme, lavender or rosemary, on the floor. Walking on them released their aromas to offset some of the bad household odors."

Margaret's interest in fragrant herbs led her to a hobby of making sachets and potpourris. The roses in her garden are her favorite fragrant varieties and their dried petals are an important ingredient in her hobby.

1. English lavender 2. Soapwort 3. Pinks 4. Sage tricolor 5. Golden thyme 6. Lemon thyme 7. Society garlic 8. Rosemary 9. Green santolina 10. Germander 11. Calamint 12. Bronze fennel 13. Curry 14. Tansy 15. Sage 16. Floribunda rose 'Cathedral' 17. Hybrid tea rose 'Fragrant Cloud' 18. Hybrid tea rose 'King's Ransom' 19. Hybrid tea rose 'Chrysler Imperial' 20. Privet.

Herbs in Containers, Indoors or Out

Container gardening creates many new garden and landscape possibilities. A container garden may be arranged and rearranged at whim. Plants can be brought close-up when at their best and returned to a staging area afterwards.

All herbs grown in containers have the same basic light, water and fertilizer requirements, whether indoors or out. But an indoor gardener works with a much narrower margin of error.

Light—Light is the most important ingredient of a successful indoor herb garden. If you have a greenhouse, greenhouse window or sun room, the kinds of herbs you can grow is unlimited. They will flourish with as little as six hours of direct sunlight a day.

If you have to use artificial light, a very simple arrangement of fluorescent lights in a basement, family room or garage is all that is necessary.

There are fluorescent lighting systems specially designed for plants, but few are so complicated or specialized that you could not rig up your own. You will need a fixture that holds two or four tubes. Fluorescent tubes that are color balanced to approximate sunlight are very good, but most herbs will do as well with a combination of cool white and warm white tubes.

Either the shelves that hold the plants or the lights should be adjustable so the optimum plant-light distance can be maintained, no matter how large the plants grow. Plant tops should be just 5 or 6 inches below the tubes. At that distance and with the lights on for 14 to 16 hours, the fluorescent lights provide all the light energy the plants need for good growth. As a rule, 14 hours of artificial light is roughly equal to 6 hours of natural sunlight.

Soil—The best soils for container plants of any kind are very porous and allow easy and plentiful air circulation. They hold a lot of water, but drain very quickly. There are many variables that affect how a plant is able to grow in a given soil, and some gardeners can make just about anything work. But for the best growth and fewest problems, use a commercial potting soil. Good ones include Jiffy Mix, Jiffy Mix Plus, Super Soil, Baccto and Metro Mix. These are lightweight, uniform in texture and disease-free. Their pH and nutrient content is properly balanced. These technicalities are

Left: A shelf for growing and storing herbs is simple to make. This one is 18 inches wide, 30 inches high and is made of redwood 1x6s. A ready-to-use, 18-inch fluorescent fixture with grow light fits under the middle shelf.

Herbs planted in box-like container, raised to table height for convenient use.

A decorative step-stand provides a setting for these kitchen potherbs.

Herbs are ideal candidates for hanging baskets. Pictured left to right are chervil, mint, parsley and chives.

more important for herbs in containers because other factors, such as light, temperature and humidity, are not as favorable and more difficult to modify.

Most commercial mixes have one or more organic components and one or more mineral components. The organic portion might be milled sphagnum peat moss, pine bark, hardwood bark or fir bark. The mineral portion might be vermiculite, perlite or fine sand. If you have several large tubs or boxes to fill, you can save money by making your own mix using the same ingredients. To make two bushels of a good container mix, use:

1 bushel milled sphagnum peat moss
1 bushel horticultural-grade perlite
10 tablespoons ground limestone
5 tablespoons single superphosphate
2 tablespoons potassium nitrate
1 teaspoon iron chelate

You can make a larger or smaller quantity by simply adjusting the proportions. Measuring bushels is easy if you keep in mind that 1 bushel is the same as 8 gallons.

Water—In the garden most herbs are drought tolerant, once their roots are deeply established. But it is a different story for an herb whose roots are confined in a container. Keep the soil evenly moist, even for rosemary and sage, two of the most drought-tolerant herbs. The mints will, of course, take as much water as you can provide, just as in the garden.

Soil composition figures prominently in any watering program, and avoiding water problems is the best argument for using a loose, fast-draining soil mix. If the soil allows air to circulate, even right after a watering, you will have few problems. Simply keep the soil moist and watch the plants grow.

If you use a heavy soil, such as one containing a large percentage of garden soil, be careful with water. Check the moisture level below the surface before adding more. Use a mulch of rock, bark or unmilled sphagnum peat moss to prevent the soil surface from caking. You should also use clay pots because they allow water and air to pass right through their sides.

Fertilizer—In the garden, herbs are adept at extracting maximum value from even relatively poor soil. Their roots are tenacious and explore a wide circle of soil for the elements they need. But for plants in containers, you must provide all the elements necessary for their growth.

Most commercial soil mixes and the mix recipe given previously include enough nutrients for three to five months, depending on how much you water and how fast the plant is growing. A commercial mix that contains no nutrients will say so on the package. When growth slows and leaves become abnormally yellow, it is time to fertilize. But fertilizer alone can't make plants grow. Your plants will need plenty of light, good temperatures and humidity.

Any kind of fertilizer will work equally well if you follow label directions. Herbs don't need a lot of fertilizer to continue growth, and their essential oils are more concentrated if the plant is fertilized sparingly. Begin fertilizing at half the recommended strength to see if that is enough. If you overfertilize, the herb will still be usable, but the flavor or fragrance will be less concentrated.

Pests—Just as outdoors, herbs grown indoors are not very susceptible to pests. Still, an occasional mealybug or whitefly might migrate to an herb from another house plant. Don't be too alarmed and don't overreact. Rub them away with your finger or a cotton swab, rinse away major infestations with slightly soapy water or snip away the infected stem. If the plants are small enough, it is easiest to do this pest-cleaning in the kitchen sink.

HERBS IN WINTER

There is no reason why herb gardening should stop once winter arrives. Replant tender annuals in pots in August and shelter them and they will be just the right size for use by November. Move tender perennials from the garden and gradually acclimate them to the indoor climate. Some herbs are tolerant of very low temperatures, and if they're not buried in snow, you can harvest leaves throughout winter.

You can start planning your winter garden as early as August. You can begin sowing seeds of basil, chervil, coriander, dill, summer savory, sage, thyme, marjoram, chives and parsley in pots. It is possible to transplant a mature basil for winter, but it will be fairly well played out by fall. It is much better to start fresh plants for winter.

Mints, oregano and tarragon are perennials that can survive winter in the garden. But if you would like to use them fresh through winter, divide and pot them as shown on page 40, just before the first frost. Leave them outside to cool and rest for three or four weeks. Then bring them inside.

Bay, rosemary, fringed lavender, *Lavandula dentata*, Crete dittany, pineapple sage and lemon verbena are tender perennials. They will take some frost, but even their roots will be killed with temperatures in the 10° to 15° F (−9° to −12° C) range. The best way to handle these is to grow them in pots all year. Let them spend the growing season in the garden, but in their pots buried to the rims. Before frosts in the fall, lift the pots and begin the gradual acclimation to indoors.

Herbs in containers can easily be shifted between outdoors in summer and indoors in winter. Here they thrive in the light available from a window greenhouse.

It is possible to transplant herbs from the garden into pots for the indoors, but the shock and adjustment is too much for most herbs. For some tips, see page 24 where Cyrus Hyde of Well-Sweep Herb Farm tells how he prepares his plants for winter.

Perennials, such as mints and tarragon, hardy thymes and sage, should be heavily mulched with a loose material after the ground is frozen. Keep them mulched until the danger of a late frost is past. This will protect them from the worst of winter and prevent the soil from *heaving* caused by alternate freezing and thawing, which will kill plants.

Herbs to grow indoors include bay, chamomile, chervil, chives, coriander, corsican mint, dill, garlic chives, germander, ginger, hyssop, lady's mantle, dwarf lavender, lemon balm, lemongrass, oregano, parsley, peppermint, rosemary, sage, dwarf santolina, scented geraniums, summer savory, sweet marjoram, tarragon, thyme, turmeric and winter savory.

Summer care of potted herbs is easier if the pot is partially buried to reduce moisture loss. In fall, simply lift the pot and move to a protected location.

Herbs by Mail

Some of the herbs mentioned in this book are available from at least one of the following sources. Also included are sources of bulk herbs, herbal crafts and essential oils. Price of catalog, if any, is shown.

ABC Herb Nursery
Route 1, Box 313
Lecoma, MO 65540
Perennial herb plants, 25¢.

Abundant Life Seed
Foundation
Box 772
Port Townsend, WA 98368
A nonprofit corporation specializing in seeds of plants native to the North Pacific Rim. Many hard-to-find herbs. $2.00 for a 2-year membership, which includes 4 newsletters. $2.65 in Canada.

Ashby's Seeds
RR2, Cameron
Ontario, Canada K0M 1G0
Many unusual herb seeds and plants. 50¢.

Atlantis Rising
7915 S.E. Stark Street
Portland, OR 97215
Extensive list of bulk herbs.

Borchelt Herb Gardens
474 Carriage Shop Road
East Falmouth, MA 02536
Long list of herb plants. Gardens open to the public May 1 to Labor Day.

W. Atlee Burpee Co.
300 Park Avenue
Warminster, PA 18974
Very popular general garden catalog that includes common herb seeds and plants.

Caprilands Herb Farm
Silver Street
North Coventry, CT 06238
Everything for the herb gardener including plants and seeds. Catalog free with a self-addressed envelope. Beautiful gardens open 9 to 5 every day, the year-round. See page 26.

Carroll Gardens
P.O. Box 310
444 East Main Street
Westminster, MD 21157
Excellent list of perennial herb plants.

Casa Yerba
Star Route 2, Box 21
Days Creek, OR 97429
Very comprehensive list of plants and seeds. $1.00 catalog price refunded with $10.00 purchase.

Comstock, Ferre & Co.
P.O. Box 125
263 Main Street
Wethersfield, CT 06109
Well-established seed supplier with a good selection of herbs.

De Giorgi Co., Inc.
P.O. Box 413
Council Bluffs, IA 51502
General seed catalog including common and unusual herbs. 66¢ for postage.

J.A. Demonchaux Co.
827 N. Kansas Avenue
Topeka, KS 66608
Culinary herb seed. 25¢.

The Grist Mill
6 Mill Street
Wolfeboro, NH 03894
Bulk herbs and spices.

Gurney Seed & Nursery Co.
1448 Page Street
Yankton, SD 57079
Variety of seeds and plants, seasonings and herbs.

Haussmann's Pharmacy
534-536 W. Girard Avenue
Philadelphia, PA 19123
Bulk herbs and essential oils.

Hemlock Hill Herb Farm
Hemlock Hill Road
Litchfield, CT 06759
Perennial or biennial herb plants. 50¢.

Herbally Yours
P.O. Box 26
Changewater, NJ 07831
Bulk herbs and potpourri. 50¢.

Herbary & Potpourri
P.O. Box 543
Childs Holmstead Road
Orleans, MA 02653
Herb products, potpourri and a short list of plants.

Herbs 'N Honey Nursery
P.O. Box 124
16085 Airley Road
Monmouth, OR 97361
Comprehensive list of herb seeds and plants, including a long list of perennial herbs. Write for free brochure.

Hilltop Herb Farm
P.O. Box 1734
Cleveland, TX 77327
Excellent selection of plants, seeds and products. $2.00.

Hummingbird Hill Herbs
18635 Sierra Madre Avenue
Glendora, CA 91740
Crafts, plants, herb garden planning. By appointment only.

Johnny's Selected Seeds
Albion, ME 04910
Long list of vegetable and herb seeds with cultural information.

J.W. Jung Seed Co.
335 S. High Street
Box H81
Randolph, WI 53956
General garden catalog with herb seeds and many garden supplies.

Logee's Greenhouses
55 North Street
Danielson, CT 06329
Excellent source of exotic plants and rare herbs. Over 50 types of scented geraniums. $2.00.

Nichols Garden Nursery
1190 North Pacific Highway
Albany, OR 97321
A very interesting catalog with many unusual herb seeds, plants, products and books.

George W. Park Seed Co.
P.O. Box 31
398 Cokesbury Road
Greenwood, SC 29647
General garden seed catalog including common and some unusual herbs.

Pickity Place
Nutting Hill Road
Mason, NH 03048
Good list of herb seed, plants and crafts. 50¢.

Poyntzfield Herb Nursery,
By Conon Bridge,
Black Isle,
Ross-shire, Scotland
Unusual herb seeds, including the extremely hardy. Catalog 30 pence(65¢).

Putney Nursery Inc.
Box GG
Putney, VT 05346
Excellent list of culinary and aromatic herb plants, many rare. 25¢.

Redwood City Seed Co.
P.O. Box 361
Redwood City, CA 94064
Unusual vegetable and herb seeds and plants from around the world. Also has an active seed exchange to help find the unusual. 50¢ for a *Catalog of Useful Plants* plus 50¢ for a supplement published every 3 months.

Otto Richter & Sons Ltd.
Goodwood
Ontario, Canada L0C 1A0
Comprehensive list of herb seeds and books. $1.00.

The Rosemary House
120 S. Market Street
Mechanicsburg, PA 17055
A unique catalog with a long list of herb plants, books, essential oils and crafts.

Roses of Yesterday & Today
802 Brown's Valley Road
Watsonville, CA 95076
Source of fragrant roses for potpourri. Ships bare-root plants, Catalog $1.50.

Rutland of Kentucky
P.O. Box 16
Washington, KY 41096
Extensive list of herb seed plants and everything for potpourris, including essential oils and fixatives. $2.00.

Sandy Mush Herb Nursery
Route 2
Surret Cove Road
Leicester, NC 28748
Extensive list of herb plants. Special section on scented geraniums. Catalog cost of $1.00 refunded with purchase.

Smile Herb Shop
4908 Berwyn Road
College Park, MD 20740
Extensive list of herb seeds and products. Will help find the unusual if they don't have it.

Sunnybrook Farms Nursery
P.O. Box 6
9448 Mayfield Road
Chesterland, OH 44026
Extensive list of herb plants including over 30 varieties of thyme. $1.00.

Sunnypoint Gardens
Route 1
Egg Harbor, WI 54209
Extensive list of herb plants and seed including over 60 varieties of scented geraniums. 50¢.

Taylor's Herb Gardens Inc.
1535 Lone Oak Road
Vista, CA 92083
Comprehensive list of herb seeds and plants with articles on culture and recipes.

The Tool Shed Herb Farm
Turkey Hill Road
Salem Center
Purdys, NY 10578
Good list of herb plants. 25¢.

Thompson & Morgan Inc.
P.O. Box 100
Farmingdale, NJ 07727

Thompson & Morgan Ltd.
London Road
Ipswich, England IP2 0BA
General garden seed catalog with common herbs.

Vita Green Farms
P.O. Box 879
217 Escondido Avenue
Vista, CA 92083
Herb plants and seeds. Also over 20 varieties of organically grown lettuce seed.

Well-Sweep Herb Farm
317 Mt. Bethel Road
Port Murray, NJ 07865
Excellent list of herb plants and seed including many unusual and hard-to-find varieties. If they don't have it, they'll help find it. 50¢. See page 22.

Materials ready for seed starting.

Propagation

Most common herbs are easily propagated by one or more of the usual methods of plant propagation—seeds, cuttings, division or layering. Listed here are the herbs best-suited to each method. For step-by-step instructions on propagating techniques, see pages 38 to 40.

SEED

Sow these annuals indoors or outdoors after soil has warmed in spring: anise, basil, borage, caraway, coriander, dill, fennel, pot marigold and summer savory. Biennials to grow from seed include burnet, feverfew and clary sage. Perennials include catnip, sweet cicely, horehound, hyssop, lovage, marjoram, winter savory and common thyme.

Angelica seeds are short-lived, so sow them in late summer as soon as they are mature. The seeds of parsley are slow to germinate—soaking in water before planting helps. Seeds of sweet cicely require exposure to cold for good germination, so plant them in fall to come up the following spring.

CUTTINGS

Herbs that can be propagated by cuttings include scented geraniums, germander, horehound, bay laurel, lavender, lemon balm, lemon verbena, oregano, rosemary, sage, pineapple sage, santolina, sweet marjoram, winter savory, common thyme, southernwood and wormwood.

DIVISION OR LAYERING

Herbs easily propagated by division include burnet, chives, sweet flag, germander, horehound, lady's bedstraw, lemon balm, pot marjoram, wild marjoram, mints, iris, sorrel, tansy, tarragon, creeping thyme, lemon thyme, sweet violets, sweet woodruff and yarrow.

Layering is a common method for propagating thymes, santolina, lemon balm, winter savory, sages and mints.

Propagation by Seed

Outdoors—Sowing seeds in rows makes it easy to distinguish the seedlings from weeds, but broadcasting is easier, especially with tiny seeds. Herbs that do not transplant well, such as dill, fennel, borage and pot marigold, should be sown where you want them to grow. In spring, as the soil begins to warm, they will germinate and begin to grow.

In mild climates, many biennials such as coriander and parsley do best planted in fall; planted in spring they may bypass their 2-year cycle and flower too soon.

Indoors—Sow seed in 2 or 4-inch pots or flats. Use light, well-drained soil such as the soil mix described for containers on page 34, or a sterilized commercial mix that prevents seedling disease. Allow six to eight weeks for seedlings to develop to transplant size.

Sow seeds indoors in potting soil for best germination.

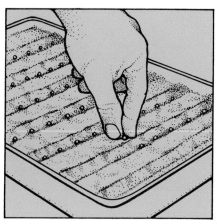

1/Plant large seeds about 1/4 inch deep with 1 to 2 inches between seeds. Firm soil. Scatter tiny seeds over firmed soil, then press into soil with flat of your hand.

2/A plastic cover or sheet of glass retains humidity and keeps seeds from drying out. Some seeds germinate best in darkness. Cover with newspaper or board.

3/Transfer seedlings to pots or, weather permitting, move larger seedlings into garden.

1/As an alternate to the above method, you can sow seeds in individual clay pots, peat pots or whatever is handy.

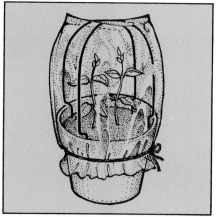

2/Cover pot with plastic bag to retain moisture for seeds and control temperature for seedlings until true leaves develop.

3/Harden seedlings in cold frame for two weeks, exposing them to chilly spring nights before transplanting.

Propagation by Cuttings

A cutting is a piece of stem that is planted like a seed. It forms roots and eventually becomes a plant identical to its parent. Cut a piece of stem 3 to 5 inches long with two or more nodes from the tip or side shoot of a healthy, well-established plant any time during spring or summer. Fall cuttings take longer to root and the stem may rot before roots form. Plant the cutting in a light, fast-draining soil mix and cover with plastic to retain humidity. Keep it out of direct sun until roots form. Check the soil occasionally to be sure it is damp but not wet. Roots will form in three to six weeks.

Root cutting—Angelica, comfrey and horseradish are propagated by root cuttings. The principle is the same, except the cutting comes from below ground and makes new shoots.

Preparing to propagate with cuttings.

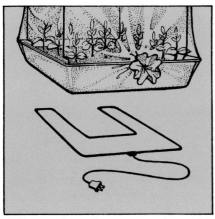

1/Make 3 to 5-inch long cuttings ending just below a leaf node. Cut off oldest leaves.

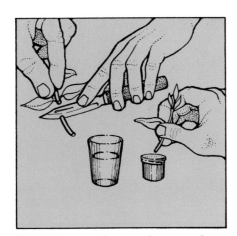

2/Hormone rooting powders speed root formation on some cuttings. Make a fresh cut on stem, moisten the base of cutting and lightly coat tip with hormone powder.

3/Soil mix for cuttings should be very porous. Use perlite alone or perlite plus small amounts of vermiculite or peat moss.

4/Bottom heat from a warming cable and high humidity provided by plastic tent ensures successful rooting of slow starting herbs like bay.

5/After 4 or 5 weeks, gently tug on the cuttings. If there is resistance, they are ready to transfer to larger pot.

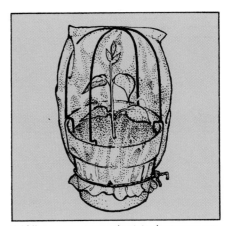

6/Allow new transplant to become acclimated for two weeks before setting outside. Plastic tent retains humidity and shades tender transplants.

Propagation by Division or Layering

These methods are generally more successful than propagation by cuttings, because the parent plant provides sustenance and moisture until new roots form.

Division: Simply dig down the middle of a clump with a shovel or trowel until you can pull away a section. Do this in spring just before the cycle of vigorous growth begins.

Layering: Any time in spring or summer, take a vigorous, flexible branch and bend it into the soil and out again. Pile soil over it and secure it with stakes or a rock. Be sure the mounded soil remains moist. Check after a month for roots. If they are present, cut the layered stem from the parent and plant.

Dividing a clump of chives.

DIVISION

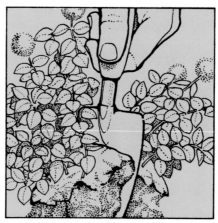

1/To divide herbs such as chives, remove whole clump of existing plant. Sprawling herbs, such as mints, can be divided by removing only a small plantable section from the soil.

2/Divide upright herbs, such as oregano and chives, by cutting out a section of the clump. For greater number of plants, make divisions smaller; for larger plants, make divisions larger.

3/Hold a clump of tarragon or chives in your hands and gently pull apart.

LAYERING

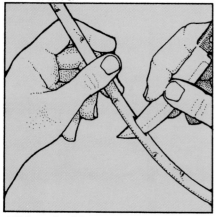

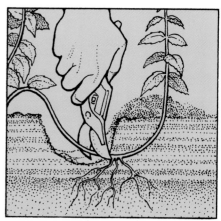

1/A long flexible stem that is close to the ground makes a good layer. Notching or wounding may speed root formation.

2/Cover stem with 3 to 4 inches of soil and hold it in place with wooden stakes or rock. Bend the growing tip vertically and support it with a stake.

3/Allow 4 to 6 weeks for roots to form, then cut off and transplant.

Transplanting

Whether purchased at a nursery or grown at home, all propagated herbs will need transplanting. Be sure they are not rootbound, old or sickly in appearance. Look for compact, stocky and vigorous plants.

Seedlings started from seeds should be transplanted when they develop their first "true" leaves—those with the characteristic shape and color of the mature herb. Handle them carefully; they have a critical area at the *neck,* the part of the stem just above the soil. A pencil, knife or similar tool will make it easier to reach under and lift the seedling's roots.

Wait until frost danger has passed in spring before transplanting, and most seedlings will benefit if you provide some shade and wind protection for a few days.

Materials needed for transplanting.

1/Develop a plan for your herb garden. Set the pots in position ready for transplanting. Keep in mind the spreading habits of some plants and the vertical growth of others.

2/Remove seedling by lightly tapping, pressing or turning the pot upside down until rootball is free. If plant is rootbound, gently pull roots apart.

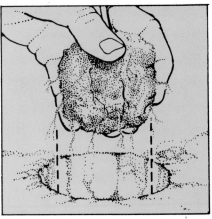

3/Make a hole large enough to accommodate rootball without bending roots.

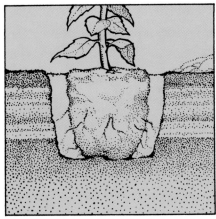

4/ Set plant at or slightly above soil line in the pot to allow for some settling.

5/Firm soil around plant just enough for it to remain upright. Too much pressing compacts top few inches of soil.

6/Water plant to settle the soil. A light mulch, some shade from sun and wind protection will aid the plant until roots are firmly established.

Herb gardening **41**

A Modern Herbal

Herbals are the oldest known writings about plants. The Chinese *Pharmacopoeia* of Emperor Shen Nung originated between 2730 and 3000 B.C., and more than 1,000 medicinal plants were described on clay tablets by Sumerians around 2200 B.C.

These earliest efforts were followed by those of Hippocrates and Dioscorides of Greece, whose combined herbal wisdom prevailed for some 1,500 years—from about 50 A.D. through the end of the medieval period.

One of the most popular herbals ever produced was written by Nicholas Culpeper in 1652. Originally titled *The English Physician,* it is generally known more simply as *Culpeper's Herbal* and was the book most consulted by the early settlers of North America.

Culpeper wrote it while in his 30's, after a short apprenticeship to an apothecary. He based his information on his own practice as an astrologer-physician. His herbal combines traditional medicine with astrology, folklore and magic. It was vigorously condemned by contemporary doctors, as it is by herbalists today, but it was loved by the people.

The encyclopedia on the following pages lists 75 herbs that are readily available and adaptable. Like old herbals, it includes brief glimpses of each herb's history, including its origins and medical and occult "powers." It also describes each herb's physical characteristics and growth habit and gives tips on its use. General how-to instructions on growing herbs begin on page 33. Harvesting and storing herbs are covered on page 120.

Many of the photographs show the herb at three stages: transplant size, six weeks later and the harvested product of each plant. These plants were provided by Taylor's Herb Gardens in Vista, California.

Though botanical names are important, in the spirit of the old herbals, we have alphabetized the herbs according to their common names. You will find a cross-reference index on page 44, giving botanical names, according to *Hortus Third,* and common names, so you can find a plant by the name you know best.

One of the best reasons for growing herbs is the pleasure they give. Bill Lathrop, husband of the author, is enjoying the rich, citrus fragrance of flowers and leaves of lemon verbena.

Herb Name Cross Reference

The herbs in the encyclopedia section of this book are listed in alphabetical order according to their most commonly used name.

You may know them by another name, so the following list is provided to help you find the herb you are looking for. Find the name you know in the first column. The name used in the encyclopedia and page number where the herb appears is in the second column.

Descriptive names are listed under the type of herb. For example, lime-scented geranium is found under scented geranium, lemon thyme is with thyme. If the common name is misleading, such as gourmet's parsley, which is actually a name for chervil, the herb is listed under the descriptive first word. Many varieties are not included on this list, but can be found in the index beginning on page 159.

Name	Page
A	
Achillea	Yarrow, 116
Acorus calamus	Sweet flag, 106
Agastache foeniculum	Anise hyssop, 48
Agrimonia eupatoria	Agrimony, 46
Agrimony	46
Alecost	Costmary, 63
Allium ampeloprasum	Garlic, 69
Allium cepa	Shallot, 103
Allium sativum	Garlic, 69
Allium schoenoprasum	Chives, 61
Allium scorodoprasum	Garlic, 69
Allium tuberosum	Chives, 61
Aloysia triphylla	Lemon verbena, 79
Ambrosia	Goosefoot, 72
American wormseed	Goosefoot, 72
Anethum graveolens	Dill, 65
Angelica	46
Angelica archangelica	Angelica, 46
Anise	47
Anise hyssop	48
Anthriscus cerefolium	Chervil, 60
Armoracia rusticana	Horseradish, 74
Artemisia abrotanum	Southernwood, 105
Artemisia absinthium	Wormwood, 115
Artemisia annua	Mugwort, 90
Artemisia dracunculoides	Tarragon, French, 109
Artemisia dracunculus	Tarragon, French, 109
Artemisia frigida	Wormwood, 115
Artemisia lactifiora	Mugwort, 90
Artemisia pontica	Wormwood, 115
Artemisia stellerana	Wormwood, 115
Artemisia vulgaris	Mugwort, 90
Asperula odorata	Sweet woodruff, 107
B	
Basil	51
Bay laurel	48
Bee balm	54
Bergamot	Bee balm, 54
Betony	Lamb's-ears, 55
Bibleleaf	Costmary, 63

Name	Page
Borage	55
Borago officinalis	Borage, 55
Boy's love	Southernwood, 105
Brassica	Mustard, 92
Burnet, salad	56
C	
Calamus root	Sweet flag, 106
Calendula	Pot marigold, 81
Calendula officinalis	Pot marigold, 81
California bay	Bay laurel, 48
Caraway	57
Carum carvi	Caraway, 57
Catnip	58
Centranthus ruber	Valerian, 114
Chamaemelum nobile	Chamomile, 59
Chamomile	59
Chenopodium	Goosefoot, 72
Chervil	60
Chinese parsley	Coriander, 62
Chives	61
Chrysanthemum	Costmary, 63
Church steeples	Agrimony, 46
Cilantro	Coriander, 62
Comfrey	62
Coriander	62
Coriandrum sativum	Coriander, 62
Costmary	63
Crete dittany	Oregano, 89
Crocus sativus	Saffron, 97
Cumin	64
Cuminum cyminum	Cumin, 64
Curcuma domestica	Turmeric, 114
Cymbopogon citratus	Lemongrass, 79
D	
Dill	65
Dusty Miller	Wormwood, 115
E	
Egyptian onion	Shallot, 103
Epazote	Goosefoot, 72
F	
Feather geranium	Goosefoot, 72
Fennel	67
Fenugreek	68
Feverfew	Costmary, 63
Fever grass	Lemongrass, 79
Finocchio	Fennel, 67
Flax	69
Foeniculum vulgare	Fennel, 67
French sorrel	104
French tarragon	Tarragon, French, 109
G	
Galium odoratum	Sweet woodruff, 107
Galium verum	Lady's bedstraw, 54
Garde robe	Southernwood, 105
Garlic	69
Garlic chives	Chives, 61
Geranium	Scented geranium, 102
Germander	70
Ginger	71
Glycyrrhiza glabra	Licorice, 80
Good King Henry	Goosefoot, 72
Goosefoot	72
Gourmet's parsley	Chervil, 60
Gow choy	Chives, 61
Great mullein	Mullein, 91
Grecian laurel	Bay laurel, 48

Name	Page	Name	Page
H		**R**	
Herb O' Grace	Rue, 95	Rosemary	94
Horehound	73	*Rosmarinus officinalis*	Rosemary, 94
Horsemint	Bee balm, 54	Rue	95
Horseradish	74	*Rumex scutatus*	French sorrel, 104
Hyssop	75	*Ruta graveolens*	Rue, 95
Hyssopus officinalis	Hyssop, 75		
		S	
I		Saffron	97
Iris germanica florentina	Orris root, 92	Sage	97
		Salad burnet	Burnet, salad, 56
J		*Salvia*	Sage, 97
Jerusalem oak	Goosefoot, 72	*Sanguisorba minor*	Burnet, salad, 56
Johnny-jump-up	Viola, 114	Santolina	100
		Santolina chamaecyparissus	Santolina, 100
K		*Satureja*	Savory, 100
Knitbone	Comfrey, 62	Savory	100
		Scented geraniums	102
L		Sesame	103
Lad's love	Southernwood, 105	*Sesamum indicum*	Sesame, 103
Lady's bedstraw	54	Shallot	103
Lamb's-ears	55	Shisho	104
Lamb's quarter	Goosefoot, 72	Smallage	Lovage, 81
Laurus nobilis	Bay laurel, 48	Soldier's woundwort	Yarrow, 116
Lavender	76	Southernwood	105
Lavender cotton	Santolina, 100	Spearmint	Mint, 83
Lemon balm	78	*Stachys*	Lamb's-ears, 55
Lemongrass	79	Staunchgrass	Yarrow, 116
Lemon verbena	79	St. John's plant	Mugwort, 90
Levisticum officinale	Lovage, 81	Sweet bay	Bay laurel, 48
Licorice	80	Sweet cicely	105
Linum usitatissimum	Flax, 69	Sweet flag	106
Lovage	81	Sweet marjoram	Oregano, 89
		Sweet woodruff	107
M		*Symphytum officinale*	Comfrey, 62
Marigold, pot	81		
Marjoram	Oregano, 89	**T**	
Marrubium vulgare	Horehound, 73	*Tanacetum vulgare*	Tansy, 108
Matricaria recutita	Chamomile, 59	Tansy	108
Melissa officinalis	Lemon balm, 78	Tarragon	109
Mentha	Mints, 83	*Teucrium*	Germander, 70
Mints	83	Thyme	111
Monarda didyma	Bee balm, 54	*Thymus*	Thyme, 111
Mugwort	90	Top onion	Shallot, 103
Mullein	91	*Trigonella foenum-graecum*	Fenugreek, 68
Mustard	92	*Tulbaghia violacea*	Garlic, 69
Myrrhis odorata	Sweet cicely, 105	Turmeric	114
N		**U**	
Nepeta	Catnip, 58	*Umbellaria californica*	Bay laurel, 48
O		**V**	
Ocimum	Basil, 51	Valerian	114
Old man	Southernwood, 105	*Valeriana officinalis*	Valerian, 114
Oregano	89	*Verbascum*	Mullein, 91
Oreganum	Oregano, 89	Violet	114
Orris root	92	*Viola*	Violet, 114
Oswego tea	Bee balm, 54		
Our lady's bedstraw	Lady's bedstraw, 54	**W**	
		Winter sweet marjoram	Oregano, 89
P		Woodruff	Sweet woodruff, 107
Pansy	Viola, 114	Wormseed	Goosefoot, 72
Parsley	93	Wormwood	115
Pelargonium	Scented geraniums, 102		
Pennyroyal	Mint, 83	**Y**	
Perilla frutescens	Shisho, 104	Yarrow	116
Petroselinum crispum	Parsley, 92	Yerba buena	Savory, 100
Pimpinella anisum	Anise, 47		
Poterium sanguisorba	Burnet, salad, 56	**Z**	
Pot marigold	81	*Zingiber officinale*	Ginger, 71

Angelica: from the nursery, after six weeks, harvested leaves and stalks.

Angelica flowers appear the second season.

Agrimonia eupatoria

AGRIMONY

Dye, tea, ornamental

This wide-spreading perennial, sometimes called *church steeples* because of its tall flower spikes, grows 2 to 3 feet tall. It makes a handsome border for other tall herbs and wildflowers.

Leaves are dark green and downy and branch very slightly. Tiny, bright yellow flowers sheath the stalks in summer and early fall.

Agrimony contains a small amount of *tannin*, and was once used in leather production. Herbalists have credited it with various curative powers, using it to treat diseases of the liver, skin and throat.

How to Grow—Sow seed or plant cuttings in spring or fall. Plant in partial shade in dry, well-drained soil. It will self-sow once established, or collect seeds from dry flower spikes.

How to Harvest and Store—Harvest leaves just before flowers open. Dry flowers and leaves by hanging whole stalks upside down.

How to Use—Reputed to make a good spring tonic. After drying, the entire plant can be ground and used for tea as discussed on page 142. The leaves, stems and flowers will produce a yellow dye as shown on page 153.

Angelica archangelica

ANGELICA

Culinary, flavoring, tea, fragrance

This large, stately herb looks tropical, but does best where it is cool and moist. It is hardy enough to have adapted well throughout Europe to north of the Arctic Circle. Its spectacular, yellow-green flowers appear in large umbrella-like clusters. They were said to bloom on the feast day of the Archangel Michael, giving rise to its name. Another theory attributes its name to the legend that an angel gave the plant to man as a cure for plague.

Ancient herbalists claimed that chewing the roots of angelica would cure numerous diseases and protect against evil and witchcraft. Modern herbalists consider angelica a tonic and stimulant.

Technically, angelica is a biennial, producing foliage the first year, flowers the second. If you cut the flowers before they open, the plant will usually last a third year—but you sacrifice the color display that lasts from May to fall. It grows to 6 feet high and 3 feet wide. It has stout, hollow stems that are purple at the base. Dark green leaves are 2 to 3 feet long and divide into smaller, glossy, toothed leaflets.

How to Grow—Angelica is occasionally available in small containers at nurseries. You can grow it from seed, but the seed is short-lived and must be planted immediately after it matures.

Plant in partial shade in rich, moist soil that is well drained and slightly acid. If soil tends to be dry, water frequently. Cultivate periodically to improve air circulation around roots and to reduce weed competition from other plants. Propagate with root cuttings and offshoots taken during the second year.

How to Harvest and Store—Pick seeds when ripe and use immediately. Harvest leaves before plant begins to flower. Dry in shade to preserve color and scent. Dig roots in late summer of second year. Cut stems in early summer of second year.

How to Use—All parts of angelica are aromatic and all parts are used. In the United States candied angelica has been used as a cake decoration. Stems can be used in salads, blanched and combined with rhubarb, preserved or candied, see page 141. Leaves can also be used in salads or cooked with fish or poultry. The roots are used for tea. Oils extracted from seeds are used for fragrance and flavor. All parts are best used fresh.

Leaf of angelica

Pimpinella anisum
ANISE
Culinary, tea

An aromatic, penetrating and warming herb with the strong flavor of licorice, anise is best known today for the liqueur it flavors. It came to the United States in the 18th century, when, according to law, each settler to Virginia had to bring and plant six anise seeds. Early Romans valued it as a condiment, cough suppressant, poison antidote and digestive aid. The 11th-century English sweetened their beds with anise sachets. Today, Orientals chew it as a breath freshener.

Anise is also pretty in a garden. A relative of parsley, this bright green annual grows to 2 feet tall. Lower leaves are broad and lobed, upper ones thin and feathery. Tiny cream-colored flowers in umbels appear in midsummer; seeds are dry by fall. Ripe seeds, which appear only during very warm summers, are gray-green. Native to the Middle East.

Anise flowers

Silver king artemisia

How to Grow—Plant anise seeds after frost in spring where you want them to remain; anise doesn't transplant easily. It likes full sun, light soil, generous and regular watering. Keep clear of weeds. When plants are 4 inches high, thin to 6 to 8 inches apart, in rows 2 feet wide.

How to Harvest and Store—Pick leaves when fully mature. Collect seedheads when they begin to change color. Hang in warm, dry place; thresh when dry.

How to Use—To make an eye-opening tea said to stimulate digestion and relieve hay fever and cold symptoms, steep 1/4 ounce seed to 3 cups water or use 1-1/2 to 3 tablespoons of chopped leaves to 3 cups water. For cooking ideas, see page 127.

Agastache foeniculum

ANISE HYSSOP

Ornamental, culinary, fragrance

An erect perennial with anise-scented flowers and leaves. Outstanding ornamental with showy, violet flowers in late summer and attractive, gray-green foliage.

How to Grow—Grow from seed or division in full sun.

How to Harvest and Store—Harvest leaves and dry.

How to Use—Anise hyssop leaves are used in teas, fruit salads, drinks and potpourris. Flowers are sometimes used in dried arrangements.

ARTEMISIA

The genus *Artemisia* is a large group of plants. It includes some very popular and useful herbs, as well as many superbly ornamental perennials and shrubs. Luckily for the herb gardener, some artemisias fall into both categories—useful in the kitchen and beautiful in the garden.

Basically, there are four types of artemisias that every herb gardener should know. They are the lemon-scented southernwood, *A. abrotanum*; the beautiful silver-gray wormwoods of several species and varieties; the indispensible kitchen herb, French tarragon, *A. dracunculus*; and the mugworts, *A. vulgaris, A. lactiflora* and *A. annua*.

Each is discussed in detail in this section, listed by its common name.

Border of Roman wormwood, an artemisia.

Laurus nobilis

BAY LAUREL, SWEET BAY, GRECIAN LAUREL

Culinary, ornamental, dye

The aromatic leaves of this attractive shrub or small tree are used to improve cooking around the world. It is an excellent ornamental, most often found in formal gardens and on patios as a close-up, well-groomed specimen plant.

Native to the Mediterranean, the compact, conical bay laurel is a slow-growing evergreen that can become a 50-foot tree. It is usually kept 2 to 8 feet tall by persistent shearing and picking. Its shiny, dark green leaves are 2 to 4 inches long, oval, thick and leathery. Small clusters of yellow flowers are followed by 1/2 to 1-inch purple berries that attract birds. Don't confuse bay laurel with the California bay, *Umbellaria californica,* especially in cooking. Leaves of the California bay are three times stronger in flavor.

Deeply entrenched in history and mythology, this is the laurel ancient Greeks used in wreaths to crown victorious warriors and athletes. When scholars receive their baccalaureate, they are winning "berries of the laurel."

How to Grow—Because it's so slow to start from seed or cuttings, it is best to purchase an established container plant. In warm climates, plant in partial shade. In cool climates, it will stand full sun. It needs good drainage. Once established, it asks for little care beyond occasional watering.

If you have cold winters, grow bay laurel in containers indoors in a cool, well-lighted spot. In summer you can move it outdoors to partial shade. Summer or winter, it appreciates humidity.

How to Harvest and Store—Harvest leaves any time, but young ones are tastiest. Hang branches from their base in a warm, dry place, or spread leaves in drying boxes. Press leaves to avoid curling. Store whole leaves in airtight jars away from light and heat.

How to Use—Bay leaves are used in a wide variety of kitchen recipes, especially dishes that must simmer for a while, such as stews, spaghetti or pot roasts. Bay leaves are also added to marinades and sauces, though in small amounts because of their pungency. See page 127 for additional culinary ideas.

Perhaps because the tree is disease and pest resistant and supposedly protects nearby plants as well, its leaves have a reputation for repelling fleas, lice and moths and even bugs that hatch in flour and grains. European cooks often put bay leaves in their rice canisters.

Bay leaves also produce a pale green dye.

Sweet bay

Sweet bay leaves

Ocimum basilicum

SWEET BASIL

Ocimum basilicum

BASIL

Culinary, ornamental

Bring indoors

Many cooks, especially Italians, feel that if they were put on a desert island with only one herb, it would have to be basil.

Ocimum is from a Greek verb that means "to be fragrant." Early Greeks considered it the herb of kings. To the Romans basil was a symbol of love; it is still called *kiss-me-Nicholas* in some areas of Italy. The French call it *herbe royale* and Hindus in India regard it as holy. *Ocimum sanctum,* listed in some catalogs as *Tulsi basil,* is India's sacred variety.

But basil's reviews have not all been complimentary. The Greek physician Galen held that it was "not fit to be taken inwardly." Culpeper, the herbalist, thought it attracted and even bred scorpions wherever it grew. Early physicians recommended that it should be planted with a great display of screaming and cursing to ensure a healthy plant and household. Hence the French expression *semer le basilic*—seeding the basil—for ranting and raving. In Salem, Massachusetts, in the late 1600's, a kitchen garden or pot containing basil was strong evidence that the grower was a witch.

Native to India and Asia and cultivated there for more than 5,000 years, basil is grown as a perennial in warm, tropical climates. A member of the mint family, most basils reach about 2-1/2 feet tall and about as wide. Tapering bright, light green leaves are 1 to 2 inches long. Creamy flowers appear in summer, in whorls on the ends of branches. Basil is almost as aromatic in the garden as in a simmering pot. Easily bruised, the tender leaves send forth sweet, pungent odors as people brush by.

If you expect to use a lot of basil, consider planting the common variety or the miniature as an annual border.

Sweet basil, *O. basilicum,* grows 2 to 2-1/2 feet tall. Leaves are 2 to 3 inches long, wrinkled and bright green. Flowers are white. This is the most commonly grown basil.

Lemon basil, *O. basilicum* 'Citriodorum', has a compact growth to 2 feet, and is lemon scented.

Lettuce leaf basil, *O. basilicum crispum,* is an import from Japan. Its large, crinkled leaves are 3 inches long, shiny and bright green. Flowers are white. Many herb gardeners report this is an excellent basil to grow indoors near a bright window or under artificial lights.

Purple basil, *O. basilicum* 'Dark Opal', has reddish purple leaves and rose-pink flowers. It will color vinegars red.

Miniature basil, *O. basilicum* 'Minimum', is much smaller and more compact than sweet basil. Other

Sweet basil: from the nursery, after six weeks, harvested leaves.

Bush basil

Purple basil

Purple basil flower stalk

common names include bush basil, French basil and sweet-fine basil. It grows to 12 inches high. Leaves are 1/2 inch long and bright green. Flowers are white. Given proper light, this is a good indoor plant.

Tree basil, *O. gratissimum,* is a shrub that grows as high as 6 feet. Leaves are 4 inches long. Flowers are pale yellow. This is an attractive ornamental and is used in cooking the same way as other basils.

Camphor basil, *O. kilimandscharicum,* is native to eastern Africa and is a 5 to 10-foot perennial shrub. Leaves are downy on both sides and smell strongly of camphor. It has been valued as a primary source of camphor for which it has been commercially cultivated.

Tulsi or sacred basil, *O. sanctum,* is a 1 to 2-1/2-foot perennial shrub. It is available in various forms—they may have purple flowers, purple and white flowers, purple or green leaves. This plant is sacred to the Hindu people and is commonly grown around their temples. It has a strong clove odor that some people believe is mildly intoxicating. Fresh leaves are used in salads or other cold dishes but never in cooking.

Like most other popular kinds of herbs, many unusual varieties are sometimes available. Other popular basils include Portuguese basil and Puerto Rican basil.

How to Grow—Basil grows easily from seed, and nursery seedlings are readily available. Plant in full sun and well-drained but moist soil. Set seedlings about 2 feet apart to allow for growth. Pinch mercilessly to encourage new growth and bushy plants. Pick off flowers as they form to promote foliage production.

How to Harvest and Store—Fresh is best, because it is most pungent. Summer crops must be preserved for winter use, and basil dries and freezes well. For peak flavor, pick whole branches just before flowers bloom.

To dry, hang upside down in a paper bag. Be careful; basil is delicate. Suspend the sprigs in a warm, dry place. You can also dry sprigs on trays or between layers of salt.

To freeze, wash whole sprigs and store in plastic bags. Press out air before freezng. Thawed basil does not look as attractive as fresh leaves, but it will taste as good. For more about harvesting and storing, see page 120.

How to Use—In the garden, either the regular or miniature basil is suitable as an annual border.

In the kitchen, basil is a king. Use it to flavor soups such as minestrone or fresh tomato. It is excellent with green peas, beans and other vegetables. Basil is an absolute must in Italian cuisine—lasagna, spaghetti, pizza and, of course, delicious pesto sauce.

Camphor basil

Lemon basil

Miniature basil

Portuguese basil

Puerto Rican basil

Tulsi or sacred basil

Bee balm

Galium verum

BEDSTRAW, LADY'S

Dye, ornamental

This pretty perennial is a close relative of sweet wood-ruff and a member of the madder family. It will grow to 3 feet tall, but can be cut back to form an interesting ground cover. Fragrant yellow flowers appear in clusters above feathery foliage from middle to late summer. It has a tendency to become a weed if not controlled, but looks very natural in a rock garden.

Originally called *Our Lady's Bedstraw*, it was probably once used to stuff mattresses. It is said to have been part of the straw that the Christ child slept on. It was used as a hair dye in Tudor England. Because the plant contains a chemical that curdles milk and is the source of a yellow to red dye, the Scots use it first to curdle milk to make cheese, then to color it.

How to Grow—Propagate by seed or rhizome division in spring or fall. Prefers full sun or filtered light and well-drained, average soil. You can allow plants to sprawl, or stake them with twine to form hoops. Roots can be divided after plants are established. Severe root pruning is recommended to keep plants under control.

How to Harvest and Store—Harvest flowers in summer after they bloom. Hang them upside down in bundles to dry. Harvest roots in fall while dormant so you do not interrupt summer growth.

How to Use—Use flowers fresh or dry as filler for flower arrangements. The roots produce an orange-red dye similar to madder *(Rubia tinctorum)*. Stems and leaves produce yellow dye. See page 153.

Monarda didyma

Cut foliage back after blooms in fall.

BEE BALM, BERGAMOT, HORSEMINT, OSWEGO TEA

Ornamental, floral arrangements, tea, culinary

A native American herb, bee balm was a favorite tea of the American Indians. It is an outstanding addition to any garden, with large, bright red flowers and fragrant leaves that emit a rich, citrus-like scent. Plant it with other favorite cutting flowers. Be aware that it is very attractive to bees and hummingbirds.

Considered a hardy perennial, bee balm grows 3 to 5 feet high in bushy clumps. Its 6-inch, dark green leaves are oval, pointed and slightly rough. They are the plant's most fragrant part. Brilliant red flowers bloom from midsummer to fall and appear in clustered whorls of frilly tubes.

Other varieties offer different colored flowers:

'Croftway Pink' bee balm

'Croftway Pink', 'Violet Queen' and 'Snow White' are popular.

How to Grow—Propagate by division or cuttings in spring or fall. Like mint, bee balm does best in moist, rich soil. Plant in partial shade and give each plant room to spread. Cut foliage back after bloom in the fall.

Dig up every three years to divide and replant. This helps control its rapid spread. Cut flower heads before they bloom the first summer to increase bloom size.

How to Harvest and Store—Harvest leaves in late summer when foliage becomes unattractive. Leaves can be dried on drying trays or by hanging them in bunches upside down by their stems. Pick fresh leaves or flowers throughout summer.

How to Use—Cut flowers are long lasting and spectacular in arrangements. Use leaves fresh or dry in tea, potpourris and salads.

Stachys byzantina

BETONY, LAMB'S-EARS
Ornamental

Lamb's-ears is another attractive herb that at one time was known medicinally but now serves as an ornamental. Its close relative betony, *Stachys officinalis,* is not as appealing, but also fits in this class.

Lamb's-ears main attraction is its woolly, silvery white foliage. It forms a low mat ideal for edging or border. It also produces stalks 12 to 18 inches tall with whorls of small purple flowers. Grow it in full sun or partial shade and well-drained soil. Some people keep the flowers cut off to favor the foliage. Others use the flowers in dried arrangements.

Borago officinalis

BORAGE
Ornamental, culinary, tea

Borage is a tough, drought-resistant annual. It was valued in ancient times for its tasty young leaves. Today it is grown for its remarkably bright, clear blue flowers.

Plants usually reach 2-1/2 feet high and 1 foot wide. Self-sown plants tend to be more robust and larger than transplants. Leaves are 4 to 5 inches long, gray-green, covered with stiff hairs. Star-shaped blooms appear in clusters on branched stems from midsummer to first frost. They are pink at first, then turn clear blue.

Borage has long been associated with courage, which may have some basis in fact. The plant contains

'Violet Queen' bee balm

Betony

Lamb's-ears

Borage: from the nursery, after six weeks, harvested leaves and flowers.

Borage flowers

a considerable quantity of potassium in the form of nitrate of potash, which stimulates the adrenal glands.

How to Grow—Borage is so easy to grow it may become a pest, though usually a welcome one. It tolerates poor soil and scant water, but it flourishes in porous, somewhat alkaline soil with moderate, but consistent water. It likes full or filtered sun.

Sow seeds about 20 inches apart once soil warms in spring. Or plant root cuttings in sandy soil in late summer, holding them through winter in a cold frame or greenhouse.

How to Harvest and Store—Pick fresh, young leaves before they become too coarse. Use both leaves and flowers when fresh—they lose flavor with drying. Leaves can be frozen in plastic bags.

How to Use—The blue flowers add beauty and are valued as cooling additions to summer drinks, desserts and salads. Scattered over a dish of sliced tomatoes, they are attractive and add a slightly bitter, cucumber flavor. Small plants and young leaves on older plants resemble spinach and are fine cooked as greens. The bristly hairs dissipate in cooking. Finely cut leaves make a delicious summer sandwich mixed with cream cheese and mayonnaise. Flowers and leaves make lovely cake or cookie decorations when candied. See page 141. Fresh blossoms brewed in water make a mildly spicy tea.

Poterium sanguisorba

BURNET, SALAD

Culinary, ornamental

Attractive as a low-growing perennial border in a garden's foreground, salad burnet has leaves that taste and smell like cucumber. It is a lovely plant and is commonly used in salads and to flavor French dressings.

Bushy, lacy leaves make salad burnet a very decorative herb. It grows close to the ground, usually no higher than 2 feet. The dark green leaves are sharply toothed, similar to those of the wild rose. Green flowers with crimson-red styles appear along stalks from midsummer to fall.

Native to the Mediterranean region, it later adapted to Asia and to Britain, where it was used as a fodder plant and in knot gardens. The Pilgrims brought it to America, where it does well everywhere except the Gulf Coast. It is the *pimpernella* in old French and Italian cookbooks. The Dutch call it *hergottes berdlen*, God's little bird, because of the featherlike foliage. Once a familiar plant in kitchen gardens, an early herbalist recommended it be planted in paths with thyme and mint, "to perfume the air most delightfully, by being trodden on and crushed." The generic name, *poterium,* is Greek for drinking cup; they used it to flavor wine, "to which it yeeldeth a certaine grace in the drinking."

It has been used as a treatment for melancholy, wounds, skin irritations and plague. The Tudors used it for gout and rheumatism.

How to Grow—Salad burnet prefers light, average, well-drained soil. Plant in the fall from seed or root division of established plants. Give full sun. Thin seedlings to 6 inches, and divide plants each year. Although tolerant of drought, it should be watered regularly. Self-sows freely, but can be prevented by removal of spent flower heads. Large plants do not transplant well. Grows well in containers.

How to Harvest and Store—Pick leaves for use after the plant is established, usually when it's at least 4 inches high. Drying destroys flavor. Better used fresh or frozen.

How to Use—Salad burnet is delicious added to salads and salad dressings. Try it chopped in herbal butters and vinegars or as a flavoring in cream cheese. Also refreshing in summer drinks.

Salad burnet: from the nursery, after six weeks, harvested leaves.

Carum carvi

CARAWAY

Culinary

The history of caraway spans thousands of years. It is well-known today for the flavor its seeds give cakes, cookies and rye bread. The plant is attractive, almost dainty, and has the fragrance of caraway throughout its roots, stems and leaves.

Caraway is a biennial, meaning it needs two seasons to complete its life cycle. The first year, bright green, carrot-like leaves form in a mound to perhaps 2-1/2 feet high. The leaves die to the ground in the fall, but a large, edible root similar to parsnip remains. The following spring, leaves reappear followed by flowers in early summer. Flowers are arranged in umbrella-shaped clusters and are white or pink. Seeds ripen about a month after flowers appear, after which the plant begins to die.

Although caraway is indigenous to all parts of Europe, Siberia, Turkey, Persia, India and North Africa, it is commercially cultivated only in relatively small areas in England, Holland and Germany. It is one of the chief agricultural crops in these regions.

How to Grow—Sow seed in spring or in early fall in mild winter areas. Soil should be loose and well drained. Water regularly. Rows of plants should be 3 feet apart with 8 to 12 inches between plants. Because

Salad burnet

Catnip: from the nursery, after six weeks, harvested leaves.

Catnip   Catnip flower stalk

of its taproot, caraway does not transplant well. Although caraway dies after its second season, enough seeds usually fall to the ground to start new plants.

If your soil freezes in winter, mulch roots heavily after soil is frozen. Pinch flower stalks as they develop and plant will live another season, growing larger with a much heavier root system.

How to Harvest and Store—Clip off seedheads when they start turning brown. Place heads in a paper bag and hang in a warm, dry place. Thresh seeds when loose and store in an airtight jar.

How to Use—Use seed sparingly. Crush to release full flavor before adding to vegetables and salads. Caraway adds flavor to breads, cheese, apple pie, cabbage and sauerkraut, brussels sprouts, cauliflower, pickles, soup and goulash. For a special treat, lightly dip raw apple slices into crushed caraway seeds.

Nepeta cataria

CATNIP

Tea, dye, cat toys

The richly aromatic foliage of catnip is, of course, a magnet to cats. If plants aren't guarded, resident and neighboring kitties will either mow them down or tear them up in their pleasure. Catnip seems to make cats either euphoric or zany; no one knows why. Appropriately, catnip is supposed to repel rats.

For people, a cup of catnip tea is either soothing or bracing. According to herbalists, a gentle person who chews catnip roots takes the risk of becoming fierce.

The variety *Nepeta faassenii* has mounding growth to 2 feet high and aromatic, gray-green foliage and lavender flowers. *N. cataria* 'Citriodora' is lemon scented.

How to Grow—

"If you set it, the cats will eat it,
 If you sow it, the cats won't know it."

As this old rhyme indicates, if you sow catnip from seed, cats supposedly won't bother it as much as they would if it were transplanted. Catnip reseeds very easily and can become a pest if not controlled.

Plant in spring or late fall in a rich, sandy soil with partial shade to full sun. Propagate by root division, seeds, layering or stem cuttings. Cut back severely throughout summer. Seeds are viable for 4 to 5 years.

How to Harvest and Store—Pick branches throughout summer after flower buds form. Dry in bunches or dry leaves in trays. Store in jars for future use.

How to Use—An enjoyable, soothing tea can be brewed from fresh or dried leaves. Tea from dried leaves is more potent.

The entire plant produces a soft yellow to gold dye. See page 153.

If you're lovingly foolish about cats, stuff dried or fresh leaves into tiny pillows or into cloth mice.

Chamaemelum, Matricaria and Anthemis

CHAMOMILE
Tea, ornamental, cosmetic

Chamomile is one of the oldest and most favored garden herbs, and has long been regarded as one of the best medicinal herbs. It was believed that its presence in the garden would keep other plants healthy. Shakespeare's Falstaff remarks, "The more it is trodden on the faster it grows." In medieval times chamomile was used as a strewing herb. It is still used today in hair rinses, perfumes, and, of course, tea.

Translated from Greek, *chamomile* means ground apple. It refers to the pleasant, apple-like scent given off by its leaves when crushed.

Native to the Mediterranean and western Europe, it is a mat-forming, evergreen perennial that reaches a height of 2 to 4 inches, but often mounds to 12 inches with age. Its light green, aromatic leaves are finely segmented. They are borne on creeping stems that root as they spread. In summer it produces small, yellow, button-like flowers. Hardy to −20° F (−29° C).

Roman chamomile is very versatile in the landscape. It can be used as a ground cover on a large or small scale. It can be mowed and used as a lawn substitute. Planted between stepping stones, it provides sweet fragrance with every step. Chamomile is also perfectly adapted to a rock garden and as a perennial border, but it can be invasive and should be kept trimmed.

Hungarian or German chamomile, *Matricaria recutita*, is a heavily blooming annual similar to *Chamaemelum nobile* in most respects but grows to a height of 15 inches or more, flowers more prolifically and makes a sweeter, more pleasantly flavored tea. It is also not as versatile in the garden.

Yellow chamomile or dyer's chamomile, *Anthemis tinctoria*, is a wonderful ornamental. Its flowers yield a yellow dye.

How to Grow—Grow chamomile from seeds sown directly in the ground, from transplants commonly available in nurseries or by divisions of established plants. Space plants 8 to 12 inches apart. Provide full sun or very light shade in well-drained but moist, light soil.

How to Harvest and Store—Flowers should be harvested when open. They can be used fresh and dried.

How to Use—Dried flowers are used to make a favorite herbal tea that is taken as sedative or for feverish

Roman chamomile: from the nursery, after six weeks.

Dyer's chamomile

German chamomile

German chamomile is preferred for tea.

Chervil: from the nursery, after six weeks, harvested leaves.

colds. German chamomile is preferred for its tea flavor. Chamomile also has many cosmetic uses and may be included in potpourri.

Anthriscus cerefolium

CHERVIL

Culinary

Chervil is an attractive addition to any garden, thriving among annuals, tidy as an edging, or handsome in a container. Similar in appearance to parsley—it is often called *gourmet's parsley*—it has a milder flavor with a slight taste of anise.

An annual, it is native to parts of Europe and Asia. Chervil grows 1 to 2 feet high, 8 to 14 inches wide. Leaves are finely cut and dark green. Small white, umbrella-like flowers bloom in clusters in summer.

In medieval times, the roots and leaves were used in salads as we use lettuce, and chervil is still a favorite salad herb of the French. It was thought to improve the humor, shake the memory and restore youth. According to Culpeper, the dried leaves were used in compresses to heal bruises. At one time vinegar laced with chervil seeds was thought to cure hiccups.

How to Grow—Chervil is usually grown from seed sown directly in the ground because young plants are difficult to transplant. Sow in late fall or early spring in filtered shade and good soil, and provide lots of water. Thin seedlings to 9 to 12 inches apart. Plant several crops two weeks apart to ensure a constant supply.

The leaves are most flavorful during cool weather and just prior to flowering. With the onset of summer, chervil begins to produce flowers at the expense of leaves. To promote leaf production, pinch flowers off before they open. Leave a few flowers and your chervil will reseed itself readily when those flowers mature.

How to Harvest and Store—You can usually begin harvesting the leaves 6 to 8 weeks after planting. The youngest leaves, picked before the plant begins to flower, will be the most flavorful. Harvesting can continue throughout the summer if you pinch off flowers before they bloom. Chervil can be dried and frozen for storage.

How to Use—Chervil is the most delicately flavored ingredient in *fines herbes* with parsley, chives and tarragon, and is a key ingredient in *béarnaise* sauce and vinaigrette.

It is an excellent addition to salads, soups and marinades, and combines nicely with butter for a chicken or fish baste.

The flavor of chervil dissipates quickly when cooked, so it is best when added just before serving. Fresh chervil has the best flavor.

Allow chervil flowers to mature for self-seeding.

Allium schoenoprasum

CHIVES

Culinary, ornamental, floral arrangements

Native to most of the Northern Hemisphere, chives are the smallest member of the onion family. The thin, hollow, grass-like leaves are dark green. They form clumps up to 1 to 2 feet tall. Chives are perennial, grown both indoors and out. The leaves are used in cooking for their mild onion flavor.

Early in the summer, small, round, pinkish purple flower heads appear on stalks above the foliage. These produce small black seeds by the summer's end. Chives will reseed themselves.

Chinese or garlic chives, *Allium tuberosum,* also known as *gow choy,* is an interesting variety with a mild garlic flavor. It is slightly larger than chives, with flatter leaves and white flowers.

How to Grow—Plant in full sun or partial shade in early spring in an average-to-rich, moist soil. Grow chives from seed or by dividing clumps of established plants. Divide clumps every 3 to 4 years and cut back plants severely and frequently. Remove flower stalks after they bloom.

How to Harvest and Store—Harvest leaves five weeks or more after planting. Use them fresh, frozen or dried. Freezing chives is a great way to store the abundance of leaves produced from one summer's growth. Clip leaves at their base, wash and chop into small pieces. Store in a container and freeze. Use whenever needed. Leaves do not have to be thawed first.

How to Use—In the garden, place chives about 1 to 1-1/2 feet apart to make an attractive border for other culinary herbs. Bulbs have a mild onion taste, but the leaves are the most useful part.

Fresh or dried flower stalks make interesting floral arrangements and filler. The flowers themselves are tasty and very attractive in salads.

Symphytum officinale

COMFREY

Ornamental, dye

The large, oblong, softly fuzzy, dark green leaves of comfrey make it an interesting and attractive addition to an herb garden. This perennial will always attract some favorable comment.

Comfrey grows in a clump and reaches a height of 3 feet. Comfrey will die back in cold weather, but reappears in the spring. Grow in full sun or partial shade from transplants or root cuttings. Cut back severely

Chives: from the nursery, after six weeks, harvested leaves and flowers.

Chive flowers

Garlic chives

Chive flowers are attractive to honey bees.

Comfrey

in winter and remove root offsets to keep plant neat and somewhat restricted. Comfrey seems to attract snails.

Use is largely ornamental. Comfrey was once used to reduce the swelling and inflammation caused by wounds and broken bones. For this reason, it was given the name "knitbone." Virginity was believed to be restored when one bathed in an infusion of comfrey. Fresh leaves and roots produce a yellow and orange dye.

CAUTION: Internal use of comfrey may be unsafe.

Coriandrum sativum

CORIANDER, CILANTRO, CHINESE PARSLEY

Culinary

Only the seeds of this versatile herb are known as coriander. Its leaves are known as cilantro or Chinese parsley. Its use dates back to Biblical times. Today the seeds are used in everything from pastries to sausage. The leaves, which resemble parsley, are the main seasoning in many Chinese, Mexican and Mediterranean dishes.

Native to Asia Minor and parts of the Mediterranean, cilantro is an erect annual usually producing one main stem 12 to 30 inches high. Young leaves are oval with toothed edges. Mature leaves are feathery and not used in cooking. They are quite pungent. Flowers are pinkish white to lavender and borne in small, umbrella-like clusters in midsummer.

The Bible compares coriander seed to manna, which fell from heaven to feed the children of Israel. The seed was placed in ancient Egyptian tombs and used by Roman soldiers as a meat preservative. Its name comes from the Greek word *koros,* which means *bedbug* and refers to the odor of the plant, which reminded our ancestors of the insect.

How to Grow—Grow coriander from seed sown directly in the ground in spring. Because of its taproot, cilantro seedlings transplant poorly. Seeds germinate quickly and can be spaced 2 to 3 inches apart. For a continuous supply of seeds until frost, make successive sowings 2 to 3 weeks apart.

Coriander prefers full sun or partial shade and a moderately rich soil with good drainage. Tall stems might need staking.

How to Harvest and Store—You can begin harvesting young leaves when the plant reaches about 6 inches high. Pick from the top 2 or 3 inches to ensure rapid new growth.

Comfrey is long-lived, eventually forming a large clump.

The leaves can be kept fresh in the refrigerator for a week or so if the stems are placed in water. Cover the tops with a plastic bag to contain the aroma.

Seeds should be harvested as they ripen in late summer. If left on the flower heads too long, they are likely to fall to the ground or be scattered.

Scald seeds to protect them against insects during storage. The method most often used is to uproot the entire plant, scald in boiling water and bag dry. Once seeds have been scalded, they cannot be used for planting in the garden.

How to Use—Ground seeds have flavor similar to orange and are used in pastries, sausages, pickling spices, cooked fruit, ground meat, salads and as an important ingredient of curry powder.

Fresh leaves are used in many Mexican, Mediterranean and Chinese dishes. The flavor is distinctive and strong, so use with caution. Try it in *salsa, guacamole,* soups, salads, stews or in stir-fry cooking in a wok. Cilantro sautéed with butter, lemon juice and garlic is delicious over prawns.

Chrysanthemum balsamita

COSTMARY

Culinary, aromatic, ornamental

This hardy perennial grows to a height of 24 to 36 inches. It bears long, narrow, light green leaves that are aromatic and have toothed edges. Clusters of yellow flowers borne on erect stems appear in midsummer.

It is a plant with many names. The name *costmary* comes from the Latin *costus,* meaning an Oriental plant, and *Mary,* referring to the Virgin Mary with whom the plant is often associated. It is also known as alecost because of its early use in making ale, and as bibleleaf because it served as a bookmarker in Bibles. Costmary was also used as a strewing herb.

Feverfew, *C. parthenium,* is a prodigious, flower-producing relative of costmary. It is perennial, aggressive and self-sows, so it tends to grow like a weed, though perhaps a friendly one. Use it for an herb garden border, or simply to add color and character.

How to Grow—Start costmary from seed or divide and replant its rhizome. It grows best in full sun and in any well-drained soil. When grown in shade, it is less likely to flower but the foliage is more attractive. In cold winter areas, it dies to the ground in fall but resprouts the following spring.

Costmary is not the most attractive plant in the herb garden. It has a tendency to get rather leggy and weedy looking. Frequent clipping will keep it looking best. It spreads rapidly by underground rhizomes and

Collect coriander seeds from mature flowers.

Costmary

Feverfew

should be divided every three or four years to keep under control.

How to Harvest and Store—The oils in its leaves are strongest just before flowering. Leaves can be used fresh or dried.

How to Use—The flavor of the costmary leaf can be overpowering. Use it only in small quantities. Try it in soups, on poultry or lightly sprinkled over salad. It can also be added to potpourris or used as a strewing herb.

Cuminum cyminum

CUMIN
Culinary

Cumin is a member of the carrot family and a cousin to caraway. It is a rather frail-looking herb whose seeds are a main ingredient in curry powder and hot, spicy dishes around the world. It requires hot summers to mature the seeds.

An annual herb native to Egypt, cumin has delicate, dark green leaves that are similar in appearance to fennel or parsley. It grows 8 to 12 inches high and 4 to 8 inches wide. In midsummer cumin bears pinkish white flowers in small umbrella-like clusters.

Cumin signified cupidity for the Greeks, but in Germany brides and grooms carry it to symbolize faithfulness.

How to Grow—Cumin is more demanding than most herbs. It needs at least three months of high temperatures for the seed to ripen.

Start cumin from seed sown in spring. If you have cool or short summers, start seed indoors and set plants outside after the danger of frost has passed. Plant in full sun and give plants plenty of space—at least 18 inches. Crowding from weeds or other plants will reduce chances for success. The soil should be light textured and drain well.

How to Harvest and Store—Uproot the whole plant just before seeds ripen to keep them from scattering. Hang the plant upside down in a paper bag until seeds drop. Whole or crushed seeds can be stored in an air-tight container.

How to Use—Powdered or whole seeds have a strong, spicy taste and should be used in small quantities. It is a must for chili or spaghetti sauce and an ingredient in many Mediterranean recipes. Many recipes for marinades, pot roast and gravy require cumin. The Swiss use it to flavor cheese, and you can use it to add zing to any dish using mild cheese. Though it isn't technically a caraway substitute—the flavor is quite different—it can be used in anything caraway is good in.

Cumin powder

Anethum graveolens

DILL
Culinary

An annual herb noted for its use in making pickles, dill adds distinctive flavor to a wide range of other foods. With its lacy foliage, large flower heads and tall habit, it also makes an interesting garden subject.

Native to Asia Minor and areas of the Mediterranean, most of the commercial dill today comes from India. It usually grows to about 3 feet tall with a single, smooth, hollow stem with shiny white and green stripes. The leaves are finely divided into feathery leaflets, similar to fennel but darker green. Small yellow-green flowers are borne in large umbrella-like clusters up to 6 inches across. The variety 'Bouquet' is smaller.

The name comes from the ancient Norse word *dilla,* which means to lull. This is a bit of a mystery. Perhaps it was given this name because its taste is very sharp and puts the taste buds "to sleep," or because it was believed to be a protection from witchcraft. It could also be a reference to the hypnotic waving of its stems in a breeze.

How to Grow—Sow seed directly in the soil in spring. Seedlings transplant poorly. Choose a site that receives full sun and has rich, well-drained soil. Don't let it dry out. Thin seedlings to at least 18 inches apart. Sow throughout the season if a constant supply is desired. It also reseeds itself vigorously.

Dill has a tendency to get leggy and may require staking. It makes an interesting background plant.

How to Harvest and Store—Leaves have fullest flavor just as the flower heads are opening. Harvest the seedheads before they are completely ripe. This will prevent reseeding. If you prefer, ripe seeds can be harvested when they are flat and brown in appearance. Store seedheads in paper bags until seeds drop. Store seeds in airtight containers.

The best way to preserve the pleasant flavor of dill leaves is to freeze them immediately after harvesting. The flavor is just not the same when dried.

How to Use—Dill can be used to make delicious pickles, but good cooks add dill seeds and leaves to a wide range of dishes and recipes. Leaves can be sprinkled on salads, cooked vegetables, fish and sauces. Mixed with cream cheese or sour cream, dill makes an excellent vegetable dip. Dill is particularly tasty with asparagus.

The unripe seeds have been used for hundreds of years to flavor vinegar. Steep a seedhead and part of the stem in 1 pint of vinegar and strain after a week or two. See page 129 for more culinary uses.

Dill: from the nursery, after six weeks, harvested leaves.

Dill flower heads

Foeniculum vulgare

COMMON FENNEL

Foeniculum vulgare

FENNEL
Culinary

Early herbalists claimed fennel made fat people thin, improved eyesight and restored color to pale skin. In mythology, Prometheus brought fire to man in a hollowed-out fennel stalk. In 490 B.C., during the battle of Marathon, which is the Greek word for fennel, Pheidippides ran 150 miles with a sprig of fennel in hand to recruit reinforcements from Sparta. Its scientific name is derived from *foenum,* the Latin word for hay, which refers to its hay-like smell.

Three types are generally available for home gardens. Common or sweet fennel, *Foeniculum vulgare,* is grown primarily for its seeds and leaves. Florence fennel, *F.v. azoricum,* also called *finocchio* or, incorrectly, *sweet anise,* is a lower-growing, 24-inch-high form used for its stems and bulbous base. Its flavor is slightly sweeter and less strong than common fennel. Bronze fennel, *F.v. rubrum,* with its bronze colored leaves, is used as an herb as well as ornamental plant.

Fennel is a member of the parsley family and native to the Mediterranean region. Similar in appearance to dill, it grows 3 to 5 feet tall. Leaves are divided into thread-like leaflets on tall, round, hollow stems that are thick and fleshy at the base. Dense, light green foliage gradually picks up a bluish tinge as the plant matures. Yellow flowers in flat-topped clusters up to 6 inches wide bloom in late summer and early fall.

How to Grow—Fennel is usually grown from seed sown directly in the ground. It germinates easily and has a tendency to reseed itself rather vigorously. It has become naturalized in vacant lots and along roadsides in many parts of the United States.

Cool weather is essential for the formation of the bulbous base of Florence fennel, so the seeds should be sown very early in spring, or at the end of summer for a late crop. In mild winter areas, Florence fennel can be harvested all winter long.

To harvest seed and foliage of common fennel, sow in early spring. Otherwise, common fennel can be treated in the same manner as Florence fennel.

The soil should be light and drain well. The planting site should receive full sun and seedlings should be thinned to 10 to 12 inches apart. If you are planting in rows, space plants about 3 feet apart. Because it is tall, fennel should be planted in the back of a bed or used as a high border. Once the plants are about 18 inches high, they may need to be staked, especially if they are planted in a windy spot. Once established, fennel is quite drought resistant.

Fennel

Florence fennel

Bronze fennel

A new leaf of bronze fennel emerges.

How to Harvest and Store—You can begin harvesting leaves when the plant reaches about 6 inches high. Pick only the top 2 or 3 inches to ensure rapid new growth.

Seeds should be harvested as they ripen in late summer. If left in the flower heads too long, seeds are likely to fall to the ground or be scattered.

The leaves stay fresh in the refrigerator for a week or so if the stems are in water. Cover their tops with a plastic bag to contain the aroma.

The seeds of common fennel should be harvested when they turn brown. Harvest leaves just before the flowers open. They can be frozen or dried and are often powdered.

The stems and base of Florence fennel should be cut before the flowers form, while they are still tender. The bulbous base of Florence fennel should be *blanched* before harvesting. Once it is about the size of an egg, pile soil up around it so no light enters. It should be ready to harvest in about two to three weeks.

How to Use—For the Italian cook, fennel is one of the essentials. It lends its distinctive anise-like flavor to everything from salad to pasta. Its leaves, stalks and bulbs are all edible and can be prepared any way you would prepare celery. The stalks, sliced with the grain, can be boiled in water or bouillon until tender and served dressed with butter and seasonings. They can also be braised with garlic and oil.

Fennel and fish are superb partners. Add fennel to the basting sauce when broiling, or place dried stalks on top of the charcoal for memorable barbecued fish. Thinly sliced and laced with olive oil, fennel makes a delicious addition to the *antipasto* tray.

Fennel leaves are used in soups, stews, salads and marinades. The seed is a common ingredient in breads, cookies, cakes, sauerkraut and salad dressings.

Fennel tea is made by pouring one-half pint of boiling water on a teaspoonful of bruised seeds. Refer to page 142 for directions on brewing tea.

Trigonella foenum-graecum

FENUGREEK
Culinary, dye

The use of fenugreek dates back thousands of years. Europeans, Asians and Africans have used the herb for seasoning, as a medicine and as animal food. Today it is used primarily as an ingredient in curry powder.

An erect annual, 18 to 24 inches in height, its leaves are three-lobed and look somewhat like clover, but more elongated. Yellowish white flowers appear in midsummer and are followed by beaked seed pods. Each pod contains 10 to 20 squarish-shaped seeds.

As a medicinal herb, fenugreek is one of the oldest known. Early Egyptians used ground seed to cure tuberculosis, bronchitis, sore throats, fever and many other diseases. It also was thought to be an aphrodisiac. Fenugreek's use as fodder dates back to the early Greeks and Romans. It is still used in the Middle East for curries, chutneys, as a coffee substitute and in some candies.

How to Grow—Fenugreek is started from seed in spring. It should be grown in full sun and well-drained soil.

How to Harvest and Store—The seeds are harvested when mature, which is usually two to three months after flowering season. Dry seed pods in paper bags, thresh and store in jars.

How to Use—Sprouted seeds are a nutritous addition to salads. The seeds are also a source of a yellow dye.

Linum usitatissimum

FLAX
Ornamental, oil, fibers

Flax is an annual herb best known as a source of linseed oil, which is extracted from its seeds. Strong fibers taken from the plant and used to make linen and cloth. This ancient plant can be traced back 5,000 years to Egypt where it was used to wrap mummies. It was also used medicinally.

Today, there are many cultivars developed for commercial purposes—large-seed varieties for oil production and small-seed types for fibers. But these are rarely available to home gardeners. Instead, home gardeners usually grow flax as an ornamental. It grows to a height of 18 to 36 inches and produces attractive blue flowers from early summer to fall.

Grow flax from seed in full sun and well-drained soil. It makes an interesting addition to an herb border.

Allium sativum

GARLIC
Culinary

This member of the lily family has been appreciated and cultivated for centuries. When Satan left the Garden of Eden after the fall of man, onions grew up in his right footprint, garlic in his left—or so goes the legend. It is as good a theory as any because no one really knows where garlic originated.

Records indicate that the Israelites ate it in the wilderness and Egyptian pyramid slaves went on strike when it was withheld from their food. Roman athletes

Garlic flowers

Oriental garlic flowers

Society garlic

Rocombole garlic

ate it for strength, soldiers ate it to gain fierceness. As a cure-all, it might be the all-time herb champion. Pliny recommends it for 61 ailments. In Europe today, garlic juice is a favorite home remedy for colds, coughs and sore throats, and modern medical research confirms its value as a disinfectant.

Gardeners say that planting garlic with roses benefits the roses, and garlic is widely acclaimed as an insect repellent.

Garlic is a perennial. Its bulb consists of cloves held together by white paper-thin skin. Flat, gray-green, grass-like leaves grow 1 to 3 feet high. Round flower heads with clusters of white flowers project on stalks in midsummer.

Rocombole or Bavarian garlic, *A. scorodoprasum,* produces new plants at the top of its growth, much like Egyptian onion. Elephant garlic, *A. ampeloprasum,* produces giant bulbs that are much milder.

Society garlic, *Tulbaghia violacea,* is not really a garlic at all. Its flat, thin leaves are variegated violet, green and white. It grows to 1-1/2 feet and makes a beautiful border in herb gardens. It is used like garlic in soups and salads.

How to Grow—Plant individual cloves or nursery sets in full sun, early in spring or fall. A sandy, rich, moist soil is preferred. Plant bulbs to a depth of 2 inches, pointed end up, no closer than 3 inches apart. Elephant garlic should be planted about 12 inches apart. Keep free from weeds and cultivate soil around bulbs regularly.

How to Harvest and Store—Harvest bulbs when tops die down in late summer. Garlic leaves can be braided together by their dried top strands or stored in bundles. Garlic dries slowly and will keep its skin for many weeks.

How to Use—Some cooks keep peeled garlic in a jar of olive oil ready for use. But garlic is always best used fresh from the bulb. See page 130 for culinary uses.

Teucrium

GERMANDER

Ornamental

Once used extensively in medieval ornamental knot gardens and as a medicinal herb, germander is now used as a landscape shrub. In ancient herbal blends, it was thought to help cure gout and improve the mind.

There are several species. Wall germander, *Teucrium chamaedrys,* grows 1 to 2 feet high and spreads to 12 inches. The variety 'Prostratum' reaches only 5 to 8 inches high but spreads 3 feet wide. Sage-leaved germander, *T. scorodonia,* is a perennial herb with crinkly, downy leaves. It grows 1 to 2 feet high, has an odor distinctly like hops and has been used as a hops substitute in beer-making. *T. fruticans* grows 4 to 6 feet high and spreads to a width of 10 feet.

All germanders have attractive foliage and flowers in summer. They are versatile plants, adapting to any garden condition as long as the soil drains well. They can be used as hedges, edgings, borders or ground covers.

Zingiber officinale

GINGER
Culinary

Fresh or dried, the thick, gnarled roots of ginger have been a key flavoring ingredient for centuries. Though Marco Polo claimed to have discovered it in China, records indicate that builders of the pyramids ate unleavened sweet ginger cakes. It was grown in monastery gardens during the Dark Ages. In the 13th century it was so appreciated by English royalty that it became literally worth its weight in gold. Ginger supposedly has a soothing effect on the digestive system. The Chinese put candied ginger in beautiful porcelain jars and present it after meals as an aid to digestion. Ginger is known to the Chinese as *Keong*.

It grows wild in tropical rain forests, such as in Hawaii, but in most gardens it must be grown in containers so it can be brought inside in winter.

A tall perennial, 3 to 5 feet high, it spreads freely by forming a large, knobby rhizome underground. Long stems project upward from each knob to produce broad, bright green leaf blades. Yellow or white flowers bloom in dense spikes 3 to 4 inches long.

How to Grow—Early in the summer, buy fresh roots at the market. Cut it into pieces if you want several plants, or use the whole root. Select a container that is about 12 inches deep and fill it with moist, rich soil. Be sure to provide good drainage. Set the root just below the surface of the soil. Place the pot in a warm and sunny spot. To avoid root rot, water sparingly until growth develops; water well after green shoots appear. Mist to maintain high humidity and fertilize regularly. Move plants indoors or into a greenhouse for the winter; they become dormant and will die down. Repot yearly to accommodate growth.

How to Harvest and Store—After one year, when plant is well established, dig up roots from young sprouts. These roots are more flavorful than older ones.

Roots will keep in the refrigerator for up to three weeks. They will keep indefinitely in a jar, covered with sherry. Or you can dry the root, grind it into powder, and store it in jars. Ginger freezes well if wrapped in plastic.

Sage-leaved germander: from the nursery, after six weeks.

Wall germander makes an excellent low hedge.

Ginger fresh from the garden.

Sliced ginger, ready for use.

How to Use—Fresh ginger can be used in recipes that call for dried, but use about half the amount called for. For Oriental or stir-fry dishes, peel fresh ginger root and chop it into thin slivers. Cook in hot olive oil with green onions until flavored. Then add whatever vegetable, fish or meat you have chosen as the main ingredient and stir quickly until cooked. The Chinese use ginger to hide the strong animal tastes of meat and fish.

Young, tender shoots are delicious marinated in rice vinegar and sugar. The Japanese call this *beni-shoga.*

It is excellent in curry dishes. Try homemade gingerbread with whipped cream.

Chenopodium

GOOSEFOOT, LAMB'S QUARTERS

Culinary, ornamental

Native to Europe and Asia, many of the *Chenopodiums* have naturalized to North America, where they now grow as somewhat weedy annual or perennial herbs. Plants of this group have been used in the past primarily as medicinal herbs. *Chenopodium ambrosioides,* known as *epazote,* is commonly used in Mexican cooking.

The botanical name comes from the Greek words *chen* or *chenos,* meaning goose, and *podos,* meaning foot. Goosefoot is the common name and refers to the leaf shape. Leaves are usually smooth and triangular in shape. Tiny flowers form in dense clusters. Spinach is a member of this family. There are many species and varieties.

Lamb's quarters, *C. album,* is a prolific weed commonly seen along roadsides. It has erect, very branched growth to 3 feet. Leaves are triangular and are covered with a white, downy fuzz. Stems are often reddish. Small, green flowers produce black seeds by late summer that are said to be highly nutritious.

Used in Mexican cooking as a mild substitute for epazote, young leaves and tender shoots can be eaten cooked or raw in salads.

Epazote or American wormseed, *C. ambrosioides,* is the true, strong Mexican seasoning. A perennial native to South America, it produces erect stems to about 2 feet tall. Leaves are more oblong than triangular. Greenish yellow flowers appear from mid to late summer. Can be grown in containers. An extract known as *American wormseed oil* comes from this plant and is believed to be useful medicinally as an antispasmodic.

Good King Henry, *C. bonus-henricus,* is also a perennial. Its leaves are large, glossy and dark green. Small, greenish flowers bloom in midsummer.

Ambrosia, Jerusalem oak or feather geranium, *C. botrys,* is an annual that grows to 2 feet tall. Fragrant, feathery foliage is small and shaped like oak leaves. Feathery branches develop as the plant matures, diminishing the leaf size. Flower clusters appear in sprays from mid to late summer.

How to Grow—*Chenopodiums* generally do well in full sun or partial shade in a light, sandy soil. Propagate from seed in spring or fall. Thin seedlings to 12 inches. Can be divided in spring. Do not transplant after cutting leaves.

How to Harvest and Store—Pick leaves of epazote for seasoning throughout the summer, once plant is established. Dry leaves on trays and store in containers for later use. Pick branches of ambrosia for floral arrangements after seeds have developed. Dry branches outdoors, which develops a beautiful green color, or place fresh branches directly in a vase without water. Harvest seeds of lamb's quarters after they reach full maturity, but before they drop.

How to Use—Use epazote with Mexican black bean and rice dishes. The leaves of Good King Henry and lamb's quarters are delicious cooked or raw. Prepare as you would spinach.

Dried branches of ambrosia are lovely in floral arrangements. The feathery foliage lends itself well to other fresh or dry flowers.

Horehound

Marrubium vulgare

HOREHOUND

Culinary, ornamental

Horehound is an herb that has been used for centuries in teas as a remedy for coughs and colds. It has also been used as a poison antidote for snake, insect and dog bites, the source of its present common name. At one time it was thought to prevent scorpions, flies and spiders from entering the home and garden.

It is native to waste areas in many parts of Europe, Asia and Africa, and has naturalized in parts of the United States. A hardy, erect perennial herb 1 to 2 feet high, the leaves are crinkled, woolly and grayish green. They are borne opposite each other on square, woolly stems and have a strong aroma similar to thyme. Small white flowers appear along the stems in summer, but only after the plant is 2 years old.

Horehound can be used as a gray edging or border in the garden, but its bushy, rather rangy habit is not very attractive. Its aroma, however, is thought to discourage flies.

Black horehound, *Ballato nigra,* is closely related to common horehound, but is very strong—and to some,

Clump of black horehound

objectionable—smelling. It is grown in the same manner, and used when dried as a tea to settle upset stomachs.

How to Grow—Horehound is undemanding. It does well in poor, sandy soil and full sun, and needs little water. It is usually grown from seed sown in flats in spring and transplanted into the garden. Seedlings should be spaced about 1 foot apart. Seed can also be sown directly in the ground or divisions can be taken from existing plants.

Established plants should be trimmed in spring to keep them looking their best, especially in cold climates where frost might injure plants. Divide plants every two to three years.

How to Harvest and Store—The leaves of horehound are best fresh—the flavor and aroma diminish when dried. Harvest young leaves any time.

How to Use—The Hebrew translation of the scientific name for horehound is *marob*. It means bitter, which best describes its flavor.

Horehound ale is made from the juice of the leaves and stems, but its most common use is in cold remedies and cough syrups. Horehound candy is also a well-known children's medicine. Some say that tea made from the leaves soothes bronchitis and sore throats. The branches of horehound are attractive in dried arrangements.

Horseradish plant

Horseradish root

Armoracia rusticana

HORSERADISH
Culinary

The hot, sinus-clearing flavor of horseradish is familiar around the world. A member of the mustard family, it was called *wild radish* by the Greeks and was considered a digestive aid and a cure for scurvy, among other things. Modern doctors confirm that it is rich in vitamin C. In the Middle Ages it was used as a cosmetic to promote color and remove freckles. It wasn't used in cooking until late in the 17th century. Even then, the Germans, who started the practice of making it into a condiment for meat, valued its health-giving properties more than its flavor. Today's Europeans still believe that they are doing something good for their health when they eat horseradish.

In the garden horseradish is a perennial that is used as an annual. It forms a long, deep root and has large, shiny green leaves with toothed edges. Small white flowers in clusters top the plant in summer

How to Grow—Because the plants rarely produce viable seed, horseradish is started from root cuttings in spring. Once planted, it needs a little more attention than most herbs, but if you follow these directions you will be rewarded with the highest-quality horseradish. Plant the root cutting with the small end down and the top 2 to 3 inches below the soil surface. The soil should be loose and drain well. The plants should be spaced 12 to 18 inches apart. When the leaves reach about 12 inches high, push the soil away to expose the root and remove all but one or two of the sprouts. It is a good idea to wear gloves while performing this task as it can be irritating to the skin. Also remove the small roots along the side of the root cutting, but make sure not to disturb the main bottom roots. Push the soil back over the roots. This operation should be repeated in about four to six weeks. Horseradish spreads rapidly and can become a pest if it is not harvested each year.

How to Harvest and Store—The roots of horseradish grow fastest during late summer and fall, so harvest as late in fall as possible. The bottom of the mature root can be cut off and saved for next year's planting. Horseradish is best used fresh but can also be dried or refrigerated after grating or cutting into 1/4-inch slices. Grate it immediately after harvesting. It will last up to three months under refrigeration.

How to Use—Horseradish finds its way into many types of sauces. Combined with sour cream, it is the perfect condiment for beef or pork. Seafood cocktail sauces would not be the same without it. Try it mixed with mustard on hot dogs or German sausage with sauerkraut.

Hyssop

Hyssopus officinalis

HYSSOP

Aromatic oils, culinary, ornamental

Hyssop is one of the few herbs that is evergreen and hardy, and can be harvested all year. With attractive shiny leaves, profuse late-summer blooms and tidy habit, it is a useful garden plant, effective as a border or low hedge. Its heady fragrance attracts bees and butterflies.

Strong in both flavor and aroma, it was used by the ancients to preserve meat and as a cleaning agent. The name comes from the Hebrew *azob*, meaning holy plant. In medieval times every monastery garden included hyssop. It was believed to ward off the evil eye and purge skin spots. To the Elizabethans it was a cure for coughs, rheumatism, jaundice, toothaches and ringing ears. They also used it to kill head lice.

Hyssop grows wild throughout the United States but originated in Europe and temperate Asia. In the

Hyssop flower stalk

garden it grows to 18 to 30 inches high, and spreads 8 to 12 inches. Leaves are narrow and dark green. Tiny blue flowers bloom in abundance on long spikes from late summer to mid-fall. The variety 'Alba' has white flowers; 'Rosea', red.

How to Grow—Plant from seed in spring or late fall. It will reseed itself vigorously, or you can propagate by summer cuttings or by division. Grows best in full sun but can take light shade. Tolerates most soils as long as drainage is good. Fairly drought resistant once established. Cut back every spring.

How to Harvest and Store—Both dried leaves and flowers can be used in potpourris. Whether used for cooking, in tea or as an addition to potpourris, oils in leaves are strongest just prior to flowering and should be harvested then.

How to Use—Hyssop oils are an important ingredient in many perfumes and soaps, and its oil is one of the flavoring agents in Chartreuse liqueur. Many people consider hyssop only slightly less valuable than lavender for use in potpourris.

Hyssop was used more often in the past as a cooking herb than it is today. Its slightly bitter taste is good with meats and fish. Use with discretion in soups and stews. Tea made from the leaves has been used to treat asthma, colds, fevers and indigestion.

Green French lavender: from the nursery, after six weeks, harvested leaves.

Green French lavender flower

Lavandula

LAVENDER
Ornamental, fragrance

Remove flowers as they fade

The lavenders are queens of the scented herb garden. Their wonderfully aromatic flowers and foliage are the backbone of many perfumes, soaps, sachets and potpourris. Fresh or dried, the branches look and smell lovely in floral arrangements. As garden plants, lavender's attractive habit is not easily matched.

Wispy and delicate in detail, with ghostly gray foliage, lavenders contrast dramatically with bold green plants. They make a softly contoured edging, low border or hedge, responding to every breeze. They nest happily in rock gardens. On a hot day their oils permeate the air and attract bees.

Though lavender was used occasionally for calming nerves and "hysterick fits," curing hoarseness and soothing aching joints, its use was seldom recognized until the Renaissance. This may have been because it was associated with vanity and sensual joys rather than religious beliefs. But in Tudor England it finally came into its own, and today large industries in England and France are devoted to growing, capturing and selling its heady aroma.

Its botanical name comes from the Latin *lavare,* to wash. From earliest times, it was used to perfume bath water and was burned as incense to cleanse hospitals.

Four varieties of lavender grow well in home gardens:

English lavender, *Lavandula angustifolia,* is the most dependable and aromatic. It is shrubby and grows to 4 feet tall and about as wide. Stems are pubescent, square and woody at the base. Its narrow, gray leaves are about 2 inches long and have smooth edges. Tiny lavender flowers clothe the 18 to 24-inch stalks in midsummer. It is hardy to 0° F (−20° C). Of the available, generally adaptable varieties, 'Alba' has white flowers. 'Compacta' grows to 10 inches, spreads 12 to 15. 'Hidcote' grows to 12 inches high and has attractive, shiny foliage, deep purple flowers. 'Jean Davis' grows to 18 inches, with pink flowers. 'Munstead', a much-loved dwarf, reaches 18 inches and produces deep lavender flowers several weeks earlier than the others. 'Twinkle Pink' is 24 to 36 inches high and has large spikes of very fragrant flowers.

French lavender, *L. dentata,* is hardy only to 15° F (−10° C). It reaches 24 to 36 inches high and has gray-green leaves 1 to 1-1/2 inches long with square-toothed edges. Dark lavender flowers in short, blunt clusters bloom nearly the year around in mild climates. The variety *L.d. candicans* has larger leaves, which are brighter gray. Green French lavender has an excellent green color and produces many flowers.

Spike lavender, *L. latifolia,* is hardy to 0° F (−20° C) and grows to 2 feet high. It has broader leaves and narrower flowers in tighter formation than the other lavenders. It yields much more oil but of poorer quality.

Spanish lavender, *L. stoechas,* is hardy to 0° F (−20° C) and has a dense, compact habit. It grows 18 to 36 inches high. Leaves are only 1/2 to 1 inch long, narrow and gray. Dark purple flowers appear in early spring in tight, short spikes.

How to Grow—You can sow seeds in flats, but expect slow germination. Small plants are usually available at nurseries. Lavender can also be grown from stem cuttings and divisions.

Lavender likes full sun, light sandy soil and good drainage. Dry conditions and low soil fertility yield maximum oils.

If they become leggy, cut back after flowering. Remove flowers as they fade.

How to Harvest and Store—Although the entire plant is aromatic, the flowers have the strongest aroma. To dry, pick the stalks in midday when the oils are most concentrated. The flowers should be showing color, but not fully open. Harvest the seeds, which are also aromatic, when mature.

French lavender: from the nursery, after six weeks, harvested leaves and flowers.

French lavender

Hedge of French lavender

Lemon balm

Lemongrass

How to Use—Lavender is rarely used in cooking, but dried flowers and seeds are one of the most popular additions to sachets and potpourris. Read about making fragrant "lavender sticks" on page 149. The oils are extracted and added to soaps, perfumes and toilet waters, and are also thought to repel insects. Lavender is excellent for dried flower arrangements.

Melissa officinalis
LEMON BALM
Fragrance, tea, ornamental

Lemon balm is an easy-to-grow perennial with a delightful lemon fragrance. Honeybees love it and are supposed to be "calmed" by it.

Lemon balm is a member of the mint family and has the characteristic four-sided stems. Heavily veined, light green leaves are nettle-like, with a strong lemon scent. Plants become 2 to 3 feet high and 8 to 18 inches wide. Very small, white flowers appear in July and last through September.

Lemon balm was named *melissa*, the Greek word for bee, by the great botanist Linnaeus. At one time a tincture of lemon balm was combined with lemon peel, nutmeg and angelica root and drunk as Carmelite water. This mixture was thought to be very effective for treating headaches and obscure pains. The crushed leaves were also applied to wounds to fight infection.

The variety 'Aurea' is most ornamental. Its leaves are variegated with yellow, but that usually disappears during flowering. After flowering, cut back to promote the growth of variegated leaves.

How to Grow—Plant in rich soil and full sun, though it will tolerate some shade. Start from seeds, which germinate slowly, cuttings or root divisions. Sow seeds in spring or late summer. Take cuttings any time and divide the perennial root in fall. Lemon balm will self-sow, and roots will spread—so allow plenty of space. Occasional cutting back will promote leaf growth and keep the plant bushy and constrained.

Lemon balm is a deciduous perennial, which means the top growth will freeze to the ground with frost. The plant is renewed each spring from the roots.

How to Harvest and Store—Collect leaves and use fresh any time. Leaves to be dried are best harvested just before flowering.

How to Use—Fresh leaves impart a scent of lemon that lasts for hours on your hands or skin. Dried leaves lend the same fragrance to sachets and potpourris. Cold teas made from fresh or dried leaves are refreshing, and hot teas are thought to relieve fever and headaches. Cut stems retain fragrance and are handsome in arrangements.

Cymbopogon citratus

LEMONGRASS, FEVER GRASS

Culinary, cosmetic, tea

This wonderful lemon-scented grass is a member of a small group of aromatic grasses native to tropical Southeast Asia.

Lemongrass grows in clumps up to 6 feet high, but is usually 2 or 3 feet high. Leaves are 3 feet long and 1/2 inch wide, dark green and slightly ridged. Lemongrass rarely flowers. It is commercially cultivated in Florida for its strong, lemon-scented oil. Confectioners use this oil in making artificially flavored lemon candy. A brew made from dried leaves is a wonderful addition to bath water or hair rinses.

Some Oriental groceries sell cut plants as well as whole plants with roots.

How to Grow—Although native to tropical regions, lemongrass is easily grown as a potted plant in cooler climates if it can be wintered indoors. In warm climates it will be fine left in the garden. Propagate in spring by clump division. Before digging clumps, cut leaves down to a few inches above the root. Plant clumps in partial shade in good, well-drained garden soil. Make sure a few inches of leaf remain above soil. Water sparingly but mist leaves often. Do not over-fertilize. Trim leaves to encourage growth.

How to Harvest and Store—Cut leaves as often as desired once plant has become established. Can be cut up into pieces, then dried or frozen.

How to Use—Wonderful in Oriental dishes. Try in sauces instead of lemon for an interesting flavor change. Also good used as a hair wash to promote shine. Makes a delicious, refreshing tea.

Aloysia triphylla

Bring indoors

LEMON VERBENA

Aromatic, culinary, ornamental

In mild winter gardens of the southern and western United States, lemon verbena is an old-time garden favorite introduced from South and Central America by Spanish explorers. In colder parts of the country it is used either as an indoor/outdoor plant or as an annual herb. Wherever it is grown, its lemon-scented leaves are a delightful addition to teas, fruit drinks, main dishes, finger bowls, potpourris and sachets. Its aromatic oils are used for perfumes and cosmetics.

A hardy, deciduous or semi-evergreen shrub that grows in mild winter climates, it will stand cold as low

Lemon verbena is excellent in a container.

Lemon verbena flowers share the lemon fragrance of the leaves.

Licorice root after three years growth.

Lovage flowers

as 10° to 15° F (−12° to −9° C). Outdoors, it has an open, rather rangy form, but it grows much smaller in containers. It can be artistically pruned and trained into a small tree.

Leaves are narrow, 3 to 4 inches long in whorls of 3 to 4. They have a heavenly lemon scent. Small white flowers cluster at the ends of branches in late summer.

How to Grow—Lemon verbena can be grown from seed, but germination and initial growth are slow. It is usually propagated and sold as rooted cuttings taken off new spring growth. In mild winter climates, grow it in full sun in any good, well-drained garden soil. In colder areas, it makes a fine container plant that can be kept outdoors in summer and brought indoors in winter. It can also be treated as an annual.

When lemon verbena is brought indoors, it will lose its leaves. Keep it in a cool location and water only sparingly. In late winter it will begin new growth. At that time, cut off weak or dead growth and, if necessary, repot before moving it back outdoors.

Lemon verbena responds to pruning and pinching. But, left on its own, it needs quite a bit of space. As the plant ages, its irregular growth can become quite picturesque.

How to Harvest and Store—The aromatic oils in the leaves of lemon verbena are at maximum just before the blossoms open. However, they remain strongly fragrant through the entire growing season.

How to Use—Lemon verbena is one of the most strongly aromatic herbs in the garden. In cooking, use it as a substitute for lemon rind. Good in teas, fruit salads, jams and jellies. Makes an attractive and tasty garnish.

The clean lemon scent is a welcome addition to potpourris and finger bowls. Scatter the leaves wherever you would enjoy a fresh lemony scent.

Glycyrrhiza glabra
LICORICE
Culinary

Licorice is an ancient herb that rarely finds its way into American gardens, although seeds are available. It is grown for its roots, which are used in medicine, for flavoring and in industry. They are usually dried and powdered.

Licorice is native to the Mediterranean and southwestern and central Asia. It is grown commercially in those areas.

Grow in a rich, moist soil from seed or division. Reaches 3 feet high with interesting, divided leaves. Harvest roots in third or fourth year.

Levisticum officinale

LOVAGE
Culinary

Lovage, also known as *smallage,* is best described as a giant version of celery. All parts are useful in cooking, and its bright, shiny foliage makes it a good background plant.

Native to the Balkans and Mediterranean area, it is a herbaceous perennial than can grow to 6 or 7 feet high and 18 inches wide. The deeply divided leaves resemble celery, but are larger and more tropical looking. They also have a distinctive odor. Small yellow flowers in flat-topped clusters appear in early spring.

In central Europe, it has enjoyed some repute as a love potion. In early Greece and Rome, it was used as a medicine. As a bath herb, it cleans and deodorizes. As a food, it was once a common ingredient in green salads.

How to Grow—Sow fresh seed in fall. In very cold climates, sow indoors and plant outdoors in spring. Germination is erratic, so overseed and thin seedlings to about 3 feet apart. Lovage grows best in full sun or partial shade in moist, rich soil with good drainage. Unless you collect the seed, it will reseed vigorously.

How to Harvest and Store—Harvest leaves when young and tender and use them fresh or dried. For best flavor cut the stems just before flowers set seed. Dig roots any time and use fresh. Collect seeds when they turn brown.

How to Use—The entire plant has a flavor often compared to celery or parsley. Use leaves to flavor salads, soups, stews, vegetables, meats, poultry, sauces or mixed in *bouquet garni.* Candy or blanch the stems and eat as a vegetable. Sprinkle the seeds over meat, candy, bread or cookies. Use roots to make tea.

Calendula officinalis

MARIGOLD, POT
Ornamental, culinary, dye

The pot marigold is grown primarily for its bright orange and yellow flowers, which are produced over a long season. It is one of the most colorful annuals for a border or edging and is commonly sold in nurseries as a bedding plant. However, it also has herbal uses. The leaves and flowers, although bitter, are often added to salads and a yellow dye can be extracted from the blossoms. Medicinally, the flowers are thought to have antiseptic value and to be helpful with gastrointestinal and muscle problems.

Pot marigolds grow best in full sun and almost any soil. They reseed heavily and flower most prolifically in the cool months of spring and fall.

Pot marigold

Pot marigold thrives in cool weather.

Mentha pulegium
PENNYROYAL

Mentha
MINT
Culinary, fragrance

Mint is the flavor of summer. It offers cool and re-freshing relief on hot days. A sprig on the rim of a cool drink or a sprinkling on a fruit salad is delightful. In the garden, it pleases both the nose and the eye.

Natives of Europe, the mints are a group of upright perennials that grow 2 to 3 feet tall. Exceptions are Corsican mint and pennyroyal. Most have smooth, branching stems, although some are hairy. All have four-sided stems. Leaves are dark green, usually quite creased, round to oval, and pointed at the tip. They flower from mid to late summer, producing whorls of tiny, white to purple blooms on spikes that form the tips of the stems.

Mints have been used for centuries as antiseptics, to aid digestion, and as a remedy for flatulence. They were also used in baths to soothe and comfort. The Greeks and Romans crowned themselves with pepper-mint during their feasting and rubbed it on their tables before seating guests.

In India they still scent rooms with mint by hanging fresh bunches in front of an open window or door. It may be that future historians will write "20th century Americans used mint to brush their teeth."

In mythology, Menthé was a young nymph who caught the eye of Pluto, ruler of the underworld. In a jealous rage, Pluto's wife, Persephone, trod Menthé underfoot. Pluto was unable to control Persephone and changed Menthé into the delightful little herb to be severed and trod upon forever.

There are likely an infinite number of species and varieties of mints. They hybridize themselves easily and many of their characteristics are variable from garden to garden. Botanists are rarely able to agree on a proper name and identity of a given mint. The fol-lowing are relatively consistent in their characteristics and are commonly available.

Water mint, *Mentha aquatica*, is well-branched and 2 feet high. Hairy stems are spindly, causing the plant to sprawl. Leaves are round to oval, sometimes fuzzy. Purple flowers appear in late summer. It has strong peppermint fragrance.

Field mint or corn mint, *M. arvensis*, grows erect to 2 feet high. It has red, hairy stems and small hairy leaves that are round to oblong. Pale lilac flowers bloom from mid to late summer. Spearmint flavor.

Japanese mint, *M. arvensis piperescens*, has stems that are taller, stiffer and more erect than *M. arvensis*. It grows 2-1/2 feet high. Its dark green leaves are narrow and pointed. Pale mauve flowers appear in whorls.

Scotch mint, *M. gentilis*, has slender, erect, purplish

'Mint-the-Best' flower spike

Apple mint leaves and flowers

Orange bergamot mint

red stems to 2 feet tall. Its coarse, oval leaves are dark green and serrated. It has pale purple flowers.

Golden mint, *M. gentilis varigata*, is low and spreading to 1 foot tall. Its leaves are smooth and variegated green with yellow streaks. It has pale purple flowers and a fruity flavor.

Horsemint or hairy mint, *M. longifolia*, grows 2 to 3 feet tall. Leaves and stems are covered with whitish gray hairs. Leaves are oval, smooth on top and hairy underneath. Attractive pale purple flowers on terminal spikes appear from mid to late summer. Very aromatic.

Peppermint, *M. piperita*, has smooth, slender stems with red tinges that grow to 3 feet. Leaves are 1 to 3 inches long, light green, smooth and oblong. Dense clusters of pale violet flowers bloom in middle to late summer. Its strong menthol aroma is very cooling. A particularly flavorful variety is black-stem peppermint.

Orange bergamot mint, *M. p. citrata*, has green, branching stems tinged with red that reach 2 feet high. Leaves are round to oval, smooth and dark green with a red edge. Purple flowers in short spikes bloom from mid to late summer. Very fragrant, citrus-like scent.

Pennyroyal, *M. pulegium*, is prostrate with a creeping, matted growth from 6 to 12 inches high. Heavily branching, deep red stems support round to oval, glossy dark green leaves that are barely 1 inch long. Long spikes hold purple-red flowers. Strong mint flavor. Good in sauces but said to be toxic in large amounts. *Bring in*

Corsican mint, *M. requienii*, has prostrate growth to 1/2 inch high. Small, round, bright green leaves resemble baby's tears. Pale purple flowers appear in midsummer. Richest peppermint flavor.

Spearmint, *M. spicata*, is well branched with erect growth 2 to 3 feet high. Reddish stems. Wrinkled leaves are oval, hairless and bright green. Pale violet flowers in long spikes bloom from mid to late summer. Useful culinary mint. Very fragrant. 'Mint-the-Best' is a variety of spearmint.

Curly mint, *M. spicata* 'Crispata', grows rapidly, spreading to 2 feet high. Hairy stems tend to sprawl by late summer. Leaves are broad, dull green and very wrinkled. Spikes hold pale purple flowers. Good ground cover. Very aromatic.

Apple or woolly mint, *M. suaveolens*, has erect growth to 2 feet. Entire plant is covered with thick, whitish gray hairs. Round, gray-green leaves are 2 to 4 inches across. Pinkish white or reddish to lilac blooms appear on long, slender spikes. Apple fragrance. Good ground cover, especially for rough or difficult areas.

Pineapple mint, *M. suaveolens* 'Variegata', is more slender than *M. suaveolens* and grows only 1 foot tall. Leaves are also smaller with white and cream patches.

Whitish gray flowers bloom in middle to late summer. Pineapple fragrance when young. Becomes more minty with age.

How to Grow—Mints grow practically anywhere, but do best in moist, rich soil with partial shade to full sun. Control is a problem because they spread easily by shallow, underground runners. One way to control them is to plant inside flue tiles, which can be purchased from construction supply dealers. Sink the flues into the soil up to rim and plant the mint inside. Or use headerboards or metal strips to restrain the underground runners.

Propagate with seed, which germinates slowly, or, more easily, by dividing established plants. Cut back often and replant every two or three years to keep healthy. If your plants develop mint rust, a fungus disease that speckles the lower foliage with orange, destroy the infected parts and replant the roots in another spot.

Mints can be very domineering in the garden and will even push out other varieties of their own family.

How to Harvest and Store—Pick mint throughout summer to keep the plant healthy and under control. Dry in bunches hung upside down to retain juices, or dry leaves in trays. Fresh leaves are usually more flavorful than dried. Mint can be kept frozen in plastic bags.

How to Use—Famous for juleps, mint is a good flavoring for sauces, salad dressings and iced drinks. A wonderful soup can be made from pieces of cooked chicken, chicken broth, lemon juice and chopped fresh mint leaves. Candied leaves of applemint are an especially attractive decoration for cakes and pastries. See page 133 for cooking ideas.

Spearmint marries well with lamb, and minted apple jelly and lamb are a classic twosome. A must in Middle Eastern cookery, it is finally wending its way westward in such dishes as *tabouleth, tahini* and *falafel.*

The oil of peppermint is the usual ingredient of mint-flavored candies. Try making peppermint candy canes for an old-fashioned Christmas. Scent a room with mint by hanging it fresh in bunches in front of an open window or door, as they do in India.

Grow mint along pathways where you can enjoy its fresh, cool aroma, and where it can be mowed for easy maintenance.

A COMPARISON OF POPULAR MINTS

On the next two pages you will find photographs of many of the more popular mints. These mints grown in our test gardens were started from transplants similar to those in the small pots. They were planted into the larger size pots and allowed to grow for approximately six weeks until these photographs were taken. The cut sprigs are the parts of the plant used for culinary or fragrance purposes.

Corsican mint

Black stem peppermint

Corsican mint

Curly mint

Peppermint

Pineapple mint

'Mint-the-Best'

Pennyroyal

Spearmint

Watermint

Origanum heracleoticum

WINTER MARJORAM

Origanum
MARJORAM, OREGANO
Culinary, tea, dye, ornamental

If you have at times been puzzled by the marjoram-oregano story, don't feel alone. Both botanists and nurserymen are confused by the number of plants that look or taste like these.

Both marjoram and oregano are in the mint family and the genus *Origanum*. Marjoram is *Origanum majorana* and oregano is *O. vulgare*. Marjoram is a tender perennial and has a more delicate, sweet flavor. Oregano is a hardy perennial and has a stronger flavor.

MARJORAM

Marjoram is also known as sweet marjoram, garden marjoram, annual marjoram and knotted marjoram. It is an upright, 2-foot shrub with reddish stems and small, 3/4 to 1-1/2-inch long, fuzzy leaves. A particularly attractive form is creeping golden marjoram. It is useful in the landscape and has the same fragrance and flavor of marjoram. It is propagated by seeds usually, but also by cuttings. It is not winter hardy.

OREGANO

Oregano is also known as wild oregano and wild marjoram. It is native to Mediterranean Europe and grows to between 1 and 3 feet high. Stems are square, hairy and often purple. It is a fully hardy perennial.

Nurseries and nursery catalogs often include many varieties of common oregano. For the most part, these varieties are the result of varying climates and soils. Still it is fun to experiment and see how they will perform in your own garden.

RELATIVES AND OTHERS

Crete dittany, *O. dictamnus,* has thick, silvery, fuzzy, almost round leaves that are 3/4 inch across. Flowers are purple. It is a 12-inch-high tender perennial that is excellent in containers. Propagate by cutting. Use fresh or dry leaves for tea or seasoning.

Winter marjoram, winter sweet marjoram or pot marjoram is *O. heracleoticum.* It is almost identical to common oregano but has more and larger oil glands. Much of the dried European oregano available in the United States is from this plant.

Pot marjoram or Cretan oregano is *O. onites.* It is a tender perennial, 1 foot high and has dark green, coarse textured leaves. Flowers are lavender. Propagate by cuttings. Use fresh or dry leaves in salads, for teas or for potpourri.

The name oregano is also given to unrelated plants that share the same or similar flavor. For instance, the herb known as Cuban oregano, Spanish thyme or Virgin Island oregano is *Coleus amboinicus.* It has thick,

Sweet marjoram

Flowers of Crete dittany

Sweet marjoram: from the nursery, after six weeks, harvested leaves.

fleshy stems and leaves that are used fresh in all the ways of common oregano.

Mexican oregano is so similar to common oregano that the commercial herb trade often does not distinguish between them. It is either *Lippia graveolens* or *L. palmeri*.

How to Grow—Grow marjoram and oregano in full sun. Plant in spring in somewhat rich, light, well-drained soil. To encourage new, bushy growth, cut back before flowers appear. They can be propagated by seed, cuttings or root division. They self-sow easily. Three and four-year-old plants should be thinned or replaced by newer plants. They also grow well indoors in a sunny spot.

How to Harvest and Store—Pick leaves as needed, though flavor is best before flower clusters appear. Oregano leaves are easily dried or can be frozen. Sweet marjoram leaves do not freeze as well.

How to Use—In the garden, the oreganos make very attractive, fragrant borders. Try golden oregano as a ground cover in a sunny area or plant in containers.

The flower tops of oregano yield a reddish brown to purple dye for wool and linen, but it is not very durable.

Pot marjoram

Artemisia vulgaris

MUGWORT, ST. JOHN'S PLANT
Culinary

Mugwort is also known as St. John's plant, in honor of St. John the Baptist, who supposedly wore it for protection while traveling through the wilderness.

The common mugwort, *Artemisia vulgaris,* is usually considered a rampant weed. It has naturalized in many parts of the United States and Europe. Although

Creeping golden marjoram: from the nursery, after six weeks, harvested leaves.

its use today is limited, some of its closely related species might be of interest to the gardener.

Native to parts of Europe and Asia, mugwort is a shrubby perennial that grows to a height of 4 to 6 feet. It is sturdy and heavily branched with reddish stems. The divided leaves are dark green on top, with a silvery down underneath. It spreads vigorously by underground rhizomes and reseeds heavily. Spikes of small, yellow flowers appear in summer.

There are two other *Artemisias* commonly called mugworts: White mugwort, *A. lactiflora,* is an erect shrub, 4 or 5 feet high. It has attractive creamy white, fragrant flowers on long spikes in late summer. Dark green leaves are divided into segments and have toothed edges. Sweet mugwort, *A. annua,* is an annual that can grow to 10 feet in one season. Lacy, yellowish green leaves have a sweet, basil-like fragrance. It is used in dried arrangements and to make perfumes.

How to Grow—If you want to bring mugwort into your garden, be prepared for the effort it takes to control it. It spreads rapidly by rhizomes and reseeds prolifically. It is best grown in large, open areas, and can be started from seed, root divisions or cuttings. Give it full sun and well-drained soil. Divide rhizomes regularly to keep the plant under control.

How to Harvest and Store—Harvest leaves just before the plant flowers in early summer. Use fresh or dried. Dig roots in fall and use fresh or dried.

How to Use—The leaves are used in England to make ale and in Germany to make stuffing for the Christmas goose. Both leaves and roots are used in teas and for a variety of medical problems.

Verbascum

MULLEIN

Ornamental

There are many species of mullein, several of which grow naturally in empty lots and along roadsides throughout the United States. In the past, herbalists used mulleins for various medicinal purposes but today they are primarily known as ornamentals.

Mulleins have attractive, thick leaves that are covered with a silvery white down and arranged in a basal rosette. In summer, usually the second year after planting because many mulleins are biennial, they produce a huge spike of yellow flowers up to 6 feet tall—a dramatic addition to any herb garden.

Mulleins are usually started from seed. They are easy to grow in a warm spot requiring only full sun and well-drained soil. They do not grow in cold, wet soils.

Oregano: from the nursery, after six weeks, harvested leaves and flowers.

Mullein

Hiking in a field of mustard.

Brassica
MUSTARD
Culinary

A common sight in an open field or orchard, the bright yellow flowers of mustard are visible for miles around. A mustard preparation can be made from the dried seeds of this common field mustard, although commercial preparations are usually a blend of the seeds of black mustard, *Brassica nigra,* white mustard, *B. hirta,* and brown mustard, *B. juncea.*

Mustard grows 3 to 6 feet tall. Leaves are lobed and bristly. Tiny, yellow flowers bloom in early summer and are followed by the seed pods.

The two varieties most commonly grown and used are black and white mustard. Black mustard seed is hotter and spicier than white.

How to Grow—Sow seed in spring. It self-sows freely and will grow like a weed under almost any conditions.

How to Harvest and Store—Collect seeds in summer from tan-colored, mature seed pods.

How to Use—To make herb mustard, grind the following ingredients with a mortar and pestle: 2 tablespoons black mustard seed, 2 tablespoons white mustard seed, 1/4 teaspoon pepper, 1/4 teaspoon salt and 1/4 teaspoon dried orange or lemon peel.

Mix into a paste with 1 teaspoon each of honey and vinegar. Add 1/8 teaspoon turmeric for yellow coloring. Store in refrigerator.

Iris germanica florentina
ORRIS ROOT
Potpourri fixative

The powdered rhizome of this iris has been used for centuries as a cosmetic additive. Powdered orris root is an effective fixative for the scents of the other ingredients in potpourri. When fresh, the rhizome is practically odorless, but when dried, it has a very sweet violet odor.

It is a perennial and grows to 2 feet high. Long blade-like leaves develop from the large rhizome. Sweet-smelling flowers, white with a pale blue tinge, bloom in early spring.

How to Grow—Propagate by division of rhizomes in late fall. Plant in moist but well-drained soil in partial shade.

How to Harvest and Store—Harvest and dry the rhizome in fall.

How to Use—Peel, chop and dry the rhizome for use in potpourris and sachets. Use about 1 tablespoon for each quart of dried flowers.

Orris root

Petroselinum crispum

PARSLEY

Culinary, ornamental

Familiar as a garnish, parsley is equally attractive in the garden. It makes a beautifully textured edging or border plant, or can be planted here and there among flowers or other herbs. It is ideal for mixed flower containers and suitable for hanging baskets.

Its origins are unknown although some say it is native to the eastern Mediterranean. Greek mythology says it sprang from the blood of Archeneous, the forerunner of death. The early Greeks fed it to their chariot horses to make them run faster and wove it into wreaths to crown victorious drivers. The fact that the seed is slow to germinate might have given rise to the superstition that no parsley germinates without first traveling to visit the devil seven times. Another superstition held that, to flourish, it must be planted by a pregnant woman.

Parsley is a biennial, producing foliage the first year, flowers the second, but it is usually treated as an annual because the leaves lose their flavor when the flowers appear. It grows in a neat mound 6 to 12 inches high. Leaves are deep green, finely divided and curled. When crushed, they have a pleasant celery-like scent. Dainty flowers are greenish yellow in clusters.

Nurseries and seed catalogs supply varieties of parsley, such as 'Extra Curled Dwarf', 'Emerald', 'Moss Curled', or 'Green Velvet', all with notably attractive foliage. Plain or single parsley, also known as Italian parsley, has flat leaves that have a stronger flavor than the familiar French parsley, *P. crispum*. Hamburg, or turnip-rooted parsley, *P.c. tuberosum*, forms an 8 to 10-inch root used to flavor soups and stews.

How to Grow—You can grow it from seed, but germination is erratic—it takes anywhere from 11 to 29 days. Soaking seeds for 24 hours before planting will improve the chances for germination. If you prefer, transplants are readily available at your local nursery.

Plant parsley transplants 6 to 8 inches apart in partial shade and rich, moist soil. Do not allow plants to dry out. For a year-round supply in cold climates, grow parsley indoors under lights.

How to Harvest and Store—Pick the outer leaves as you need them, making sure you preserve the inner growing point. Leaves are best preserved by freezing. Fresh parsley will keep in the refrigerator for quite a while if the leaf ends are kept in water or if the entire leaf is wrapped in a cloth towel or kept in a special parsley bag. Hamburg parsley root can be dried like carrots.

How to Use—Parsley is a familiar garnish that adds freshness to any plate. For other uses see page 133.

French parsley: from the nursery, after six weeks, harvested leaves.

Italian parsley: from the nursery, after six weeks, harvested leaves.

Rosemary

Bring indoors

ROSEMARY

Culinary, ornamental, cosmetic

One of the oldest herbs known to man, this member of the mint family has stood the test of time in the home and in the landscape. The flavor it imparts to food is distinctive and delicious, and the sweet pinewood scent of its leaves, flowers and oils is valuable in perfumes, toiletries and sachets. In the garden, it is as useful and handsome as any ornamental.

The blue color of the flower is said to have come from the Virgin Mary, who dried her cloak on a rosemary bush, instilling in it the color of the sky. Mary is also said to have hid behind a rosemary bush when fleeing into Egypt with the baby Jesus.

Shakespeare immortalized rosemary in *Hamlet* as a symbol of remembrance and fidelity. It is an old English custom for the bride to give the groom rosemary on the wedding morning to ensure love, wisdom and loyalty; but another English saying goes, "Where rosemary flourisheth, the women ruleth."

Through the ages, rosemary has been credited with healing wounds, alleviating headaches, inducing sleep, and restoring memory, hair and youth. For years in France it was strewn on the floors of prisons and courts, and burned as incense in hospitals to prevent the spread of disease.

Though one legend claims rosemary grows only in the gardens of the righteous, it is extremely adaptable. Depending on variety, you can use it as a ground cover, hedge or foundation shrub. Prostrate forms will drape over the sides of walls or containers and are an excellent choice for hanging baskets. All types of rosemary can be easily made into bonsai.

These are some of the most notable varieties available. 'Albus' has white flowers. 'Collingwood Ingram' has gracefully curved stems. It reaches 2 to 3 feet high, spreads to 4 feet or more and is good as a tall ground cover. 'Lockwood de Forest' is low growing to 18 to 24 inches and spreading. It has light green leaves, dark blue flowers, spills nicely over walls and is an excellent ground cover. 'Prostratus', or dwarf rosemary, grows to 2 feet high, 6 to 8 feet across. It is an excellent ground cover and is nice in a hanging basket. 'Tuscan Blue' grows upright to 6 feet and has dark blue-violet flowers.

How to Grow—Rosemary can be easily grown from cuttings or divisions, or by air layering. Seed is slow to germinate, and seedlings are slow to develop. Grows best in full sun and in light, well-drained soil.

In mild winter areas, it can be grown outdoors all year, but where temperatures fall below 0° F (−20° C), grow it in containers and bring it inside in winter. Once

Rosemary drapes over a low wall next to steps.

indoors, give it good light and high humidity; dry heat causes leaf drop.

Outdoors, rosemary can take quite a bit of heat and drought once established. Water promotes growth, but the plant responds well to pruning. It does attract bees.

How to Harvest and Store— You can pick and use the leaves at any time of year, but oil is at maximum just before flowering. They can be used fresh and are easily dried or frozen.

How to Use—A long-standing natural with pork and veal, rosemary can also be used in stews, herbal butters, vinegar, jam and bread. The oil is used in perfumes and toiletries, and the leaves and flowers are valuable used in sachets and potpourris.

Ruta graveolens
RUE, HERB O' GRACE
Ornamental, culinary, dye

Beautiful, lacy, gray-green leaves make rue an interesting garden ornamental or an attractive background contrast with dark green plants. As a bonus, its musky foliage is believed to repel garden pests. Some claim it deters the Japanese beetle.

In the early Roman Catholic Church, priests used rue branches to sprinkle holy water, giving it the name *Herb O' Grace*. The generic name *ruta* means to set free in Greek. According to legend, Mercury gave it to Ulysses to free him from Circe, but the name may also refer to the belief that rue set people free from so many diseases including headache, hysteria, snake bite, fever, plague, poor circulation and even old age. It was planted near stables to repel flies and hung in rooms to repel household insects. The Chinese use it today as an antidote for poison and to fight malaria.

The ancient Greeks used it as a pungent cooking herb, and some cooks today chop it for use in sandwiches and salad dressings. Greeks also believed that the secret of getting rue to grow well in your garden was to steal it from a neighbor.

A perennial semi-evergreen, rue is native to the Mediterranean region. It grows to a height of 3 feet and is branching and woody at the base. Tiny, delicate leaves cover the entire plant, giving it a bushy appearance. Bright yellow flowers bloom from midsummer through fall and produce interesting seed pods.

Other varieties offer bluer foliage and are equally attractive in the garden. 'Blue Mound' has gray-blue foliage and more compact growth than common rue. 'Jackman's Blue' produces the richest blue leaves. 'Variegated' has leaves that are green and creamy white.

How to Grow—Rue prefers full sun to partial shade in an average, slightly acid soil, but will tolerate poor soil.

Rue

Rue attracts honey bees.

Salvia officinalis
GARDEN SAGE

Propagate in late spring by dividing established plants. Root cuttings or sow seeds after blooms fade. Thin plants to 2 feet apart.

How to Harvest and Store—Pick branches for floral arrangements throughout summer. Hang bunches upside down in a dry place. Allow seed pods to dry on plant, but harvest before they open. Seed can be removed after drying.

How to Use—CAUTION: Rue is not to be taken internally. Large amounts are toxic and particularly dangerous to pregnant women.

Foliage is attractive used as greenery in floral arrangements. Dried seed pods are also interesting additions to arrangements. Roots produce a rosy red dye.

Crocus sativus

SAFFRON
Culinary

A much sought-after and expensive flavoring, saffron is a traditional ingredient in French *bouillabaisse*, Spanish *paella* and Swedish and Cornish saffron breads. The powder is produced from the dried and crushed stigmas of the fall-blooming bulb. Expense and rarity of saffron is due to the fact that it takes a whole field of flowers to produce a tiny bit of dried saffron; 40,000 flowers are needed to make 1 pound.

Saffron grows from bulbs or, more accurately, corms. Its flower is similar to garden crocus. The large golden stigmas protrude from a blue or purple flower.

How to Grow—Saffron prefers a rich, well-drained soil in partial shade.

How to Harvest and Store—Propagate in fall by division of bulbs or corms.

How to Use—Saffron is delicious baked in homemade bread or added to rice. It imparts a lovely, warm yellow color to whatever is cooked. A little goes a long way—fortunately.

Salvia

SAGE
Culinary, ornamental, fragrance

The sages are members of the mint family and have a long tradition of medicinal importance. In fact, the word sage comes from the Latin word *salvere*, which means to be saved and refers to its alleged curing properties. A Latin proverb from the Middle Ages translates, "Why should a man die when sage flourishes in his garden?" It was a medicinal cure-all, even thought to cure baldness. In medieval times, sage was thought to impart wisdom and to improve the memory. The old English word *sage*, meaning a wise man,

Clary sage flower stalk

Cleveland sage flower stalk

comes from this belief. Superstition has it that when all is well, sage will flourish. When things are going badly, it will hang its foliage. Today, the aromatic sages are used in cooking and as prized ornamentals. Oils from their leaves go into perfume, and pineapple sage can be added to potpourris.

The sages, with all their forms, foliage colors and beautiful flowers, are excellent garden plants. Depending on variety or species, they can be used as edgings, borders or background, or as a small hedge.

Garden sage, *Salvia officinalis*, is the most common and frequently grown. It is a hardy perennial that grows to a height of 24 to 30 inches. Leaves are grayish green and oval. Violet flowers are borne on tall spikes in early summer. 'Albiflora' has tall spikes of white flowers. 'Aurea', or golden sage, has a compact habit and variegated yellow foliage. 'Purpurea', or purple sage, has leaves edged in purplish red. 'Tricolor' has variegated leaves of white, purplish red and pink.

Clary sage, *S. sclarea,* is the tallest species, reaching 4 to 5 feet high. It is a biennial that produces a basal rosette of leaves the first year and wonderful spikes of bluish white and rose flowers the second. The leaves are large, bumpy and gray-green. Seed should be sown each year to ensure flowers every season. Its common name comes from its old-time use as an eyewash: "clear eye" condensed to "clary." Its leaves also make an excellent tea.

Pineapple sage, *S. elegans,* has light green leaves with a delightfully strong pineapple fragrance. It produces scarlet flowers in fall. Pineapple sage is the least hardy variety and is usually killed at 20° F (−5° C), but it can be grown in containers and brought indoors in winter.

Blue sage, *S. clevelandii,* is a 4-foot sage native to western North America. Give it full sun, well-drained soil and virtually no summer water once it is established. It has a wonderful fragrance and is a good substitute for common sage in the kitchen.

How to Grow—Sages are generally grown from seed or cuttings. They prefer full sun and poor, well-drained soil. They are easily killed by overwatering or soggy soil, and are drought tolerant once established. Annual trimming will increase bushiness.

How to Harvest and Store—The leaves can be harvested any time and used fresh, dried or frozen.

How to Use—The sages are quite versatile. They can be used to flavor poultry or pork stuffings, sausage, cheese, egg dishes, cooked vegetables and fish. Sage oils are extracted and used to make perfumes. The leaves of clary sage can even be fried like fritters. Pineapple sage finds its way into jams and jellies and any sage can be added to potpourris and sachets. See page 134 for ideas on cooking with sage.

Golden sage: from the nursery, after six weeks, harvested leaves.

Golden sage, variegated form.

Pineapple sage: from the nursery, after six weeks, harvested leaves.

Blue sage: from the nursery, after six weeks, harvested leaves.

Tricolor sage

Sage

Santolina: from the nursery, after six weeks, harvested leaves.

Santolina with flowers

Santolina chamaecyparissus

SANTOLINA, LAVENDER COTTON

Ornamental, insect repellent

Beautiful, silver-gray foliage makes santolina a very attractive, fragrant, low-growing border. It is a native of the dry hillsides along the Mediterranean, which over the years has made it tough and drought resistant. For an interesting effect, plant it among other silvery plants, such as southernwood, wormwood and lavender.

Santolina is perennial and grows to 2 feet high. Its leaves are rows of downy, round teeth that are divided into narrow segments. Tiny, yellow, button-shaped flowers are borne on tall stalks from the stems, blooming from mid to late summer.

The leaves yield an oil used in perfume, and dried bunches hung in closets supposedly repel moths. Dried flowers are interesting in floral arrangements. These flowers were once known as *Iva flowers,* and were given to children as a treatment for worms.

How to Grow—Propagate in spring from seeds, which germinate slowly, or by plant division, layering or cuttings. Does best in full sun. Will tolerate a dry, saline soil, though it prefers a moderately rich, well-drained soil. Prune in spring to encourage growth throughout summer. Do not prune in the fall and never cut to the ground because foliage reappears on old wood. Mulch to protect roots in cold winter climates. Remove dead flowers.

How to Harvest and Store—It is best to harvest branches in late spring or early summer. Hang upside-down in bunches to dry.

How to Use—Hang dried bunches in closets to repel moths. Dried flowers are interesting in floral arrangements. Wonderful in the garden as a border or accent plant.

Satureja

SAVORY

Culinary, ornamental

Two types of savory are popular in herb gardens: summer savory, *Satureja hortensis,* and winter savory, *S. montana.* Both are planted in spring. The only difference is that summer savory is an annual and winter savory a perennial that can be harvested year-round.

Both are native to the Mediterranean and southern Europe. The Druids probably used savory in their rituals. The Romans flavored vinegar with it. Pliny planted it near his bees to improve their honey. Hippocrates valued savory's medicinal properties, and Culpeper recommended it for treating deafness and bee stings.

Summer savory is erect to 18 inches with a rather open habit. Its slim, aromatic, gray-green leaves are about 1-inch long and become tinged with purple in late summer. White to pinkish flowers in whorls clothe the stems from midsummer until frost. It makes a fine container plant and can be used in a border. The German name for summer savory is *Bohnenkraut*, which means bean herb. Many say that planting it among beans will keep whiteflies away.

Winter savory reaches 8 to 15 inches in height and its narrow leaves are smaller, stiffer and stronger in aroma than summer savory. Purplish pink flowers are borne in abundance midsummer to fall. It makes a fine edging or border plant and adapts well to a rock garden. It is even fire retardant if well watered.

Some nurseries carry *S. douglasii*, a creeping perennial and close relative to both. It is native to the west coast of the United States, where it first lent its common name, *Yerba Buena*, to the city that is now San Francisco.

How to Grow—Grow summer savory from seed sown directly in the ground, or from nursery transplants spaced 6 to 9 inches apart. It reseeds heavily and may develop weak stems that require staking.

Winter savory starts slowly from seed, and germination can be erratic. Space plants about 10 inches apart. It can be propagated more easily by cuttings or division.

Winter savory, a perennial, is hardy to about 10° F (−10° C) and should be trimmed back each spring. Its growth slows with age, so it should be replanted every four to five years.

Both savories grow best in full sun and well-drained soil. However, summer savory prefers a rich organic soil and winter savory likes a sandy and relatively moist soil.

How to Harvest and Store—Savories can be used fresh, dried or frozen. For drying, harvest just before flowering. Winter savory can be used fresh all year.

How to Use—Both winter and summer savory have a strong peppery flavor. Summer savory is usually preferred for cooking because of the texture of its leaf and more mild flavor. It can be sprinkled over salads, mixed with vegetable soup or stew or added to vinegar. It is good with poultry and an interesting addition to potpourris and sachets.

Summer savory

Winter savory

Rose geranium: from the nursery, after six weeks, harvested leaves.

Coconut geranium

Nutmeg geranium

Pelargonium

SCENTED GERANIUMS

Fragrance, ornamental, culinary

Unmatched in variety of fragrance, beautiful in the garden and a collector's dream, the scented geraniums are a large group of plants growing rapidly in popularity. There are many to choose from, each with its own distinctive habit and fragrance. Colorful flowers appear in spring, but they are generally small.

Along with a wide range of delicious scents, scented geraniums also come in a versatile array of plant forms. They can be grown in hanging baskets, window boxes or any type of container. Trailing forms can be used as ground covers, and any type is perfect for a flower border. Children are especially fascinated by scented geraniums.

Here are some of the most widely available varieties:

Rose geranium, *Pelargonium graveolens,* has spicy, rose-scented foliage. It has small clusters of pink flowers. Leaves are dark green with tiny, white hairs.

Peppermint geranium, *P. tomentosum,* is vigorous growing and spreads to a 4 to 6-foot mound. Clusters of white flowers appear in summer. Leaves are lobed and medium green. This one is ideal for a hanging basket.

Lime-scented geranium, *P. nervosum,* has beautiful lavender flowers in summer. Leaves are serrated, round and light green. Can become quite bushy.

Apple-scented geranium, *P. odoratissimum,* is another good geranium for hanging baskets. Clusters of white flowers appear on trailing stems. Leaves are round and ruffled.

Lemon-scented geranium, *P. crispum,* makes tiny, purplish pink flowers and has small, wrinkled leaves. Its clean, lemon scent freshens a room quickly.

Coconut-scented geranium, *P. grossularioides,* has a trailing habit that works nicely as a ground cover or in a hanging basket. Flowers are in small clusters. Leaves are round and dark green.

Other popular scented geraniums include: nutmeg geranium, *P. fragrans;* orange geranium, *P. crispum* 'Prince of Orange'; apricot-scented geranium, *P. scabrum* 'M. Ninon' and an almond-scented variety named 'Pretty Polly'. There are at least 50 others according to some lists.

How to Grow—Stem cuttings are the easiest way to propagate scented geraniums. Some varieties can also be grown from seed. They are not particular about soil, as long as it's well drained. They can take full sun in cool climates, but should be given partial shade in warm areas. Pinching will encourage bushiness.

Most scented geraniums are only hardy to about 20° F (−5° C). In areas with lower temperatures, bring them indoors in winter or grow in a protected spot.

How to Harvest and Store—The leaves can be harvested any time and used fresh or dried.

How to Use—Scented geraniums are of limited use in cooking, but they are used in some jellies, puddings, stuffings, punches, teas and vinegars. The oils in leaves are often distilled to make perfume, and the leaves make a sweet addition to sachets and potpourris.

Sesamum indicum

SESAME
Culinary

Sesame seeds are frequently added to salads, Oriental dishes, soups, baked goods and a wide range of other foods. Sesame oil is derived from the seeds.

The sesame plant can also be an interesting addition to the garden. It is a shiny-foliaged annual that reaches 3 feet high. It should be grown in full sun; the warmer the climate the better. Plant a lot. You will need 20 to 30 plants for a cup of seed.

Seeds are harvested four to five weeks after the flowers open. Left too long on the plant, they will scatter. Cut with a long stem attached. To dry, hang them upside down in a bag in a warm location. See page 134.

Allium cepa

SHALLOT
Culinary

Considered to be a variety of onion, the shallot differs from this large group because its bulbs freely multiply. Each bulblet produces leaves that could be considered individual plants, independent of the whole. The bulbs are perennial. Leaves grow from 1 to 2 feet tall. If planted in the spring, bulbs can be harvested in late summer. Shallots rarely flower.

Once called *eschalot,* after the ancient city of Ascalon in Palestine, its discovery has been credited to the crusaders who brought it back to Europe. French cooking wouldn't be the same without it.

A variety known as Egyptian or top onion, *Allium cepa vivaparum,* can be sown early in the spring. It grows to 3 feet. This onion seems to be upside down, with new bulblets or plants forming at the top of the leaves as a sort of crown. These bulblets eventually fall to the ground and produce new plants, but they can be used in the kitchen while young. Separate the root bulbs, as you do with shallots, in fall and plant for next year.

How to Grow—Plant in early spring from sets or nursery plants. Cover sets to twice bulb length. Prefers full sun and well-drained soil. It is best to dig up and separate bulbs at the end of the growing season and to replant the individual bulbs before winter.

Peppermint geranium: from the nursery, after six weeks, harvested leaves.

Egyptian onion

Shisho

Shisho grows to 3 feet high.

How to Harvest and Store—An old saying about shallots, "plant on shortest day, lift on longest," still applies. Harvest bulbs in late summer when tops turn brown and die down. This assures that the bulb will be fully mature.

Tie in bunches by their browned tops and hang in a dry, airy place. Store bulbs in onion bags. Be sure to save enough bulbs for next year's crop.

How to Use—For a delicious shallot butter for steaks, roasts or hamburgers, use a boiled mixture of 2 tablespoons red or white wine, 1 tablespoon chopped shallot, 1 tablespoon pan drippings and 1/4 pound melted butter. Season with chopped parsley, salt and pepper. This butter is called *buerre bercy* and is a French classic.

Perilla frutescens
SHISHO
Culinary, ornamental

Native to Southeast Asia, the seeds of shisho or perilla are used as a source of oil and the leaves as a salad herb in Korea and Japan. The leaves are cinnamon scented and are used fresh or pickled with raw fish, bean curd and sliced cucumber. A sweet flavoring is derived from seed and so is an oil used for drying paints and inks.

Shisho has adapted to many parts of the United States but is rarely appreciated. Plant is erect to 3 feet high and grows best in full sun or partial shade and well-drained soil.

How to Use—Green-leaved varieties are preferred for fresh use; the purple-leaved kinds are used as red food dye. Shisho is also an outstanding ornamental.

Rumex scutatus
SORREL, FRENCH
Culinary

The shape of French sorrel gives it the botanical name *scutatus,* which means shield in Latin. Its perennial growth is almost prostrate, only 1 to 2 feet tall. When used in salads, it imparts a tangy, somewhat citrus flavor.

Propagate by division of roots or sow seed in the spring. Plant in moist, rich soil. Prefers full sun. Best grown in containers because the plant can become a pest in the garden. Divide plants every three or four years to keep in shape. To promote leaf growth, remove flowers as they form.

It does not dry well, but can be frozen. Use fresh or frozen leaves in soups or salads.

Artemisia abrotanum

SOUTHERNWOOD

Fragrance, ornamental, culinary

Southernwood, or as it is also affectionately called, old man, lad's love or boy's love, is a must for an ornamental herb garden. It provides soft texture and fragrance with lacy, gray-green leaves that permeate the air with a wonderful lemon scent. A natural in a gray garden, it also complements other plants. It can be used as a shrubby border or small hedge if kept trimmed. It also is attractive in a rock garden.

Native to southern Europe, southernwood is a woody perennial that forms a multistemmed clump 3 to 4 feet tall. The gray-green leaves are finely divided into feathery segments. Yellowish white flowers appear in mid to late summer.

In France, southernwood is called *garde robe* because it repels moths. Women used to bring large quantities of southernwood to church because its pleasing scent was thought to prevent drowsiness. It was also considered an aphrodisiac and was thought to prevent baldness.

How to Grow—Southernwood is grown from divisions taken in spring or fall, and it roots easily from stem cuttings. Seeds are slow to germinate. It prefers full sun and well-drained, average garden soil. It tolerates poor soil and drought once it becomes established.

You can keep it clipped or trimmed to almost any size. Annual trimming is a good way to keep the plant looking full and fresh. Divide every three or four years.

How to Harvest and Store—Harvest leaves for drying any time. Pick flowers for tea just before they open.

How to Use—Leaves can be used in sachets and potpourris, and also as a moth repellent. Tea made from the leaves and flowers has been used medicinally as a stimulant, astringent and antiseptic.

Myrrhis odorata

SWEET CICELY

Culinary, ornamental

This is an excellent background plant for a wooded or shady flower garden. A member of the parsley, or *Umbelliferae* family, its seedheads resemble little umbrellas. The slightly oily seeds are deliciously spicy, with overtones of anise or licorice. The oil is used in flavoring chartreuse liqueur. Because every part of the plant is edible, it has found its way into folk medicine and has been valued highly as a potherb.

Sorrel seedheads

Southernwood

Sweet cicely is a tall perennial growing to 5 feet. Its large, delicate, bright green foliage resembles parsley. White flowers in clustered umbels appear in midsummer, ripen into seedheads by fall.

How to Grow—Plant fresh seed in the fall in rich, moist, shady soil. Sweet cicely self-sows freely once established. Transplant seedlings in spring to a spacious and shady part of the garden. Cicely can also be propagated in fall by root division.

How to Harvest and Store—Pick leaves from established plants throughout summer. Leaves do not dry well. Harvest seedheads just before they turn brown. Put seedheads in paper bags and hang to dry. Harvest roots late in fall after the plant has gone dormant or when it's time for root division.

How to Use—Add fresh leaves and seeds to salad for a unique flavor. The leaves are sweet enough to be used in pastry and are also good as tea. Sweet cicely is a natural sweetener for a diabetic diet.

Peeled root can be chopped and eaten raw in salads, or steamed. Try it stir-fried in Oriental cooking.

Use seeds in pastry and cakes or try them in apple pie. When crushed, the oily seeds can be mixed with melted beeswax and used as a scented furniture polish.

Ripening seeds of sweet cicely.

Sweet flag

Acorus calamus

SWEET FLAG

Potpourri, decorative, culinary

Also known as *calamus root*, this hardy, aquatic perennial prefers to grow in very moist, marshy conditions. Native to Asia and Eurasia, calamus has adapted to many parts of the world. The roots are used in perfumes and are added to gin and beer as a flavor smoother and enhancer.

Calamus is derived from the Greek word *kalamos*, meaning reed, which describes the foliage of this plant. Leaves are gold-green, very narrow, pointed and distinctly ridged. The whole plant is extremely fragrant with a spicy citrus scent. Grows 3 to 4 feet tall. Tiny, yellow-green flowers are borne in clusters on a short, spiked branch that curves upward directly out of the reed stalks. It flowers only when grown in water.

How to Grow—Plant rhizome division in full to partial shade in spring or fall, in moist, average soil.

How to Harvest and Store—Harvest and dry 2-year-old rhizomes in late fall. This allows the plant to develop well before dividing. Dried roots can be stored whole, or chopped and powdered. If you make it into a powder, peel the rhizome before drying. Dry leaves through the summer.

How to Use—Dried rhizomes are standard ingredients in potpourris, but you can also use dried leaves. Fresh or dried seedheads are interesting in floral arrangements. Some people recommend a tea made from the powdered root for an upset stomach.

Galium odoratum
SWEET WOODRUFF
Fragrance, ornamental, beverage

This lovely member of the madder family has beautiful, slightly fragrant, dark green foliage that seldom reaches higher than 12 inches. Sweet woodruff makes an attractive ground cover in shade. It also tolerates dry soil. The pointed leaves grow in whorls around the stems. Tiny white flower clusters appear at the end of the stems in early summer.

The "ruff" of its name comes from *rovelle*, the French word for wheel, and refers to the arrangement and texture of its leaves. Some think that the *wood* in its name refers to its belonging in deep, dark woods where it happily grows wild.

It was considered a valuable medicine in the Middle Ages for heart, liver and stomach problems, and for treating wounds.

When dried, it develops a fragrance strongly reminiscent of new-mown hay. For this reason it was one of the most favored strewing herbs in homes and churches. It was scattered about on the floor to freshen musty rooms, and stuffed into mattresses to sweeten dreams. Because of its spicy odor, it is still valued for use in potpourris and sachets, and is used commercially in perfumes and balms. It is delicious in most cold and fruit drinks, and fresh or dry leaves make a soothing tea. In Germany, it is traditional in May wine.

How to Grow—Seeds are slow to germinate. Plant or propagate by division of clumps in spring or fall. Prefers partial to full shade and a well-drained, rich soil. It is self-sowing once established, so it may become a pesky weed. If you need to restrain it, you can mow it with a rotary mower. This rough treatment will push it back some, but does no permanent harm.

How to Harvest and Store—Fresh woodruff has very little aroma, but when dried it has a wonderful, faintly vanilla fragrance. Pick stems and dry them upside down in bunches. Leaves and stems freeze well.

Sweet woodruff thrives in full shade.

Sweet woodruff is just the right height for a border.

Tansy: from the nursery, after six weeks, harvested leaves.

Fern leaf tansy: from the nursery, after six weeks, harvested leaves.

How to Use—Sweet woodruff is great in the garden as a ground cover under shrubs, such as roses, or other tall herbs. It will tend to grow over and dominate similar-sized plants. It spreads with underground runners and happily sends forth new growth between stepping stones.

May wine is a traditional drink of spring and utilizes sweet woodruff for its unique flavor. See page 140 for the recipe.

Tanacetum vulgare

TANSY
Ornamental, dye

As an herb, tansy is primarily of historical significance. In today's herb garden, it is grown as an ornamental for its attractive, dark green, fern-like foliage and bright yellow, very long-lasting flowers. Its rhizomes and leaves can be used to make dyes. Tansy, especially the variety *Tanacetum vulgare crispum*, is excellent for the herb border.

A perennial herb, tansy dies to the ground each fall and resprouts the following spring. It forms a broad clump to 4 feet tall. Its leaves are dark green, heavily divided and fern-like in appearance with a camphor scent. Small yellow, button-like flowers top the plant in midsummer.

When strewn about the home, it was thought to repel ants and flies. But it was most commonly used in medicinal tea for treating diseases ranging from plague to colic. It was also used to preserve meats. At one time, tansy cakes were awarded as prizes to winning athletes.

T.v. crispum is more decorative than the species with a deeper green, more delicate foliage and larger orange-yellow flowers.

How to Grow—Tansy can be started by seed or division. It grows best in full sun and is not demanding about soil as long as it is well drained. It spreads rather vigorously by underground rhizomes and should either be given a lot of room or divided frequently.

How to Harvest and Store—Harvest flowers as they open for use in dried arrangements and as a dye. Harvest rhizomes any time.

How to Use—CAUTION: Tansy is no longer used in teas or food because the leaves are now known to contain a toxic oil. It is particularly unsafe for pregnant women.

Rhizomes are used to make a green dye and the leaves a golden yellow dye. Both the flowers and leaves are beautiful in dried arrangements.

Artemisia dracunculus

TARRAGON, FRENCH
Culinary

French tarragon, widely known for its distinctive flavor and aroma, is an essential herb for most cooks. Do not confuse it with its close relative, Russian tarragon, *Artemisia dracunculoides*, which is almost indistinguishable in appearance, but tastes milder and much less flavorful. French tarragon is always preferred for cooking.

French tarragon can be used as a small-scale ground cover. It also grows well in containers and in hanging baskets. For a good kitchen supply, one or two plants are usually adequate. It is widely available from nurseries.

French tarragon is native to parts of southern Europe, Asia and eastern United States. It is a slow-growing perennial that spreads by underground rhizomes and grows to a height of 1 to 2 feet. The narrow leaves are shiny green and highly aromatic. Flowers are inconspicuous and sterile, if they show up at all.

The Greeks knew French tarragon as early as 500 B.C. Arabs in the 13th century called it *tarkhum,* meaning dragon, because it fought a good fight against pestilence. When it reached Europe in the 16th century the French called it *esdragon,* also meaning dragon, perhaps because the roots look like a mass of serpents, or because of its fierce flavor. Either way, "tarragon" is probably a corruption of the word *esdragon.*

How to Grow—The seed of French tarragon is sterile, so it must be propagated by division or cuttings. Divide plants in spring, or take stem or root cuttings in fall or spring.

Grow it in full sun or partial shade in rich, well-drained soil. Because it is naturally spreading, it is best to space plants at least 2 feet apart. In cold climates, it can freeze in the ground, so protect its roots with mulch. Divide plants every three to four years to keep them growing vigorously.

How to Harvest and Store—The leaves of French tarragon are most flavorful in early summer, before flowering. They are best used fresh, but can also be frozen or dried. Dried French tarragon loses its distinctive flavor quickly, so take care in packaging and storage.

How to Use—French tarragon is a versatile herb. It is wonderful with poultry and veal, and in salads, soups and seafood. Marinades shouldn't be made without it. See page 135.

French tarragon is a main ingredient in *béarnaise* sauce and green goddess salad dressing. And it can be added to white vinegar, page 136.

Tarragon

Tansy flowers

Thymus citriodorus
LEMON THYME

Thymus

THYME
Culinary, ornamental

Pronounced "time," more than 400 species of this highly aromatic, wonderful herb have been cataloged. Most are as useful in the garden as in the kitchen. Of the many species and varieties, three are commonly grown for their unique characteristics. Common thyme, *Thymus vulgaris,* is a popular kitchen herb with upright growth and woody stems. Native to Europe and Asia, it is a perennial evergreen, seldom reaching over 12 inches high. Its leaves are narrow, dark green to gray-green, and highly aromatic. Mother-of-Thyme, *T. praecox arcticus,* has low growing, spreading foliage that makes it very useful as a ground cover. Woolly thyme, *T. pseudolanuginosus,* has attractive woolly foliage and is extremely low growing.

Thymes are naturals for rock gardens. They can be walked on and make sturdy, redolent ground covers planted as garden pathways. Bees love them, and plantings around fruit trees help ensure pollination.

The Greeks believed that thyme imparted strength and fortitude. Their words for courage, *thymon* or *thumus,* might have given rise to the herb's name. Another theory is that it is a derivative of a Greek word that means to fumigate because of the plant's use as incense. The Greeks' association of thyme with courage was carried into medieval Europe. Ladies embroidered scarves showing bees hovering over branches of thyme. These were given to knights as tokens of bravery. "To smell of thyme" was one of the highest compliments one could be paid.

Thyme tea was believed to prevent nightmares. People tucked leaves under pillows to induce sleep.

Thyme belongs to the mint family and, like its relatives, is rich in volatile oils. The chief oil, *thymol,* is a powerful antiseptic and is used in lotions and salves.

Because the thymes readily hybridize and have been cultivated for so many centuries, many named varieties exist. Some authors list more than 60 varieties of specific culinary or garden value, but distinguishing characteristics may be minute.

The following varieties are the most useful ones and those commonly found in catalogs.

T. 'Annie Hall'. Creeping growth 3 inches high. Fragrant pink flowers.

T. camphoratus, 6 to 12 inches high with rose-colored flowers. Foliage strongly camphor scented.

T. caespititius, prostrate and mounding growth. White to lavender flowers and light green foliage.

Lemon thyme, *T. citriodorus.* Grows 12 inches high. Rich lemon-scented leaves, from dark green to yellow-green in color. Pale lilac flowers. A cross between

Lemon thyme: from the nursery, after six weeks, harvested leaves.

Bed of flowering lemon thyme.

Modern herbal **111**

'Narrowleaf English' common thyme: from the nursery, after six weeks, harvested leaves.

English thyme

T. pulegioides and *T. vulgaris*. Excellent culinary thyme.

Silver lemon thyme, *T. citriodorus* 'Argenteus'. Variegated silver leaves. Lemon fragrance.

Golden lemon thyme, *T. citriodorus* 'Aureau'. Green and yellow variegated leaves. Creeping growth. Lemon fragrance.

T. doerfleri. Prostrate growth with woolly, gray foliage. Pink to lavender flowers.

Loevyanus thyme, *T. glabrescens*. Low growing with fuzzy, gray leaves and stems. Purple flowers.

Caraway-scented thyme, *T. herba-barona*. Dark green leaves, matting growth. Leaves have a caraway fragrance. Rose-pink flowers.

T. nitidus. Grows 5 to 10 inches high with small, hairy leaves. White flowers.

T. nummularius. Spreading growth 8 inches high with smooth, shiny, dark green leaves. Rose-pink to purple flowers. Good low hedge or border plant.

Marschallianus thyme, *T. pannonicus*. Mat-forming, prostrate growth 3 inches tall. Long, narrow leaves. Rose-lavender flowers. Good ground cover.

Mother-of-Thyme or creeping thyme, *T. praecox arcticus*. Creeping growth 2 to 6 inches high. Fuzzy blue-green leaves. Lavender-blue flowers. Good ground cover or pathway filler.

Creeping white thyme, *T. p.* 'Albus'. Grows 2 inches high with white flowers.

Coconut thyme, *T. p.* 'Coccineus'. Glossy, dark blue-green foliage. Grows 3 inches high. Pink flowers.

Woolly thyme, *T. pseudolanuginosus*. Grows 2 to 3 inches high and has soft, woolly leaves. Excellent between paving or stepping stones.

Common thyme or garden thyme, *T. vulgaris*. Grows 6 to 12 inches tall with woody stems. Leaves are small, grayish green and pointed. White to lilac flowers. Good border plant.

Silver thyme, *T. v.* 'Argenteus'. Silver and green variegated, lemon-scented foliage.

T. v. 'Aureus'. Bright yellow and green variegated foliage.

T. v. 'Fragrantissimus'. Extremely fragrant, gray foliage.

English thyme, *T. v.* 'Narrowleaf English'. Grows 8 inches high with narrow, bright green leaves.

French thyme, *T. v.* 'Narrowleaf French'. Grows 12 inches tall with narrow, gray leaves.

How to Grow—Plant in spring in a spot with full sun and a light, well-drained soil. Winter care might be necessary in areas where freezing occurs. Protect with a mulch and press down areas heaved by frost. Plant matting and climbing varieties over rocks or on slopes.

Cut back severely in the summer to keep neat and to prevent woody growth. Water regularly in warm weather.

Can be propagated from seed, though seedlings grow slowly. Best propagated by cuttings or root division. Happy indoors in a sunny window.

How to Harvest and Store—Thyme can be cut all summer as plants mature. When plant receives its final trimming for the fall, leaves can be dried for future use. Tie thyme in bunches and hang upside down in dry place, or strip leaves from stems and dry on trays. Thyme leaves also freeze well.

How to Use—Make thyme tea by brewing one teaspoon of dried leaves in one cup hot water. It is said to relieve flatulence, calm nerves and soothe coughs and sore throats. A good tea mix is 3 parts thyme and 1 part each rosemary and spearmint.

In the kitchen, thyme is invaluable. It goes well with carrots and onions, and particularly well in meat dishes. Add dried thyme leaf to barbecue sauce. Thyme is excellent with fish and is a traditional ingredient in clam chowder. Added to marjoram, parsley, and a bay leaf, thyme becomes *bouquet garni*. See page 124.

Mother-of-Thyme: from the nursery, after six weeks, harvested leaves.

Woolly thyme

Caraway thyme

Silver thyme

Common valerian

Common valerian   Red valerian

Sweet violet

Curcuma domestica

TURMERIC

Culinary, dye

Turmeric is familiar to lovers of bread and butter pickles as the herb that gives pickles their characteristic flavor and yellow color. It is grown for its tuberous root, which is dried and ground and used as a spice, and makes a yellow dye. Tropical, it is rarely grown outdoors in the continental United States, but sometimes is grown in greenhouses. It is usually started by divisions of a rhizome taken in spring. Powdered turmeric is an essential part of curry powder and both colors and flavors many foods.

Valeriana officinalis

VALERIAN

Ornamental

Valerian is a tall, perennial herb used today primarily as an ornamental. At one time, it was used medicinally to treat almost any problem of the heart or central nervous system, including epilepsy.

Valerian grows to a height of 4 feet. It has finely divided leaves and attractive clusters of white to pinkish purple flowers. It grows best in full sun.

Red valerian, *Centranthus ruber,* is a completely different plant—an invasive perennial with the ability to hold on tenaciously in areas too dry, too steep, or too rough for other plants. Generally used as a ground cover, it has an attractive bloom.

Viola odorata

VIOLET

Ornamental, fragrance

The sweet fragrance and dramatic beauty of the violet has been admired not only by herbalists, but also by poets, artists and lovers. Its oils have been extracted for perfumes, and its leaves have been brewed for centuries to make an uplifting and strengthening tea. But today it is valued mainly as a garden ornamental by most people, and as a delightful culinary curiosity, for the color it adds to punches, wines and salad, by a few. Its dried flowers are a colorful addition to potpourris, but the fragrance is not lasting.

This low-growing, hardy perennial is an excellent choice for a colorful edging, small-scale ground cover or container plant. Leaves are dark green and heart shaped. Flowers come in shades of deep violet, bluish pink and white. It spreads by runners above ground and grows to a height of 2 to 12 inches, depending on the variety.

There are several thoughts as to the origin of the name violet. Some say it comes from the Latin *vias,* meaning wayside, where they were known to grow. Others say it stems from the Greek *Ione* because the Greek god Jupiter grew them to feed the goddess Io.

Historically, violets have been used to cure a wide range of maladies from epilepsy to depression. It has also been associated with quelling anger and inducing sleep.

Of those varieties available in nurseries, 'Royal Robe' has large, long-stemmed, deep purple flowers; 'Charm' has small, white flowers, and 'Royal Elk' has very fragrant violet flowers.

Many other species of violets are commonly grown, including many popular garden annuals and perennials, such as pansies and Johnny-jump-ups, *Viola tricolor.* Some, such as Johnny-jump-ups, have their own herbal histories, usually associated with medicinal uses.

How to Grow—Grow from seed, runner division or nursery transplants. Partial shade is ideal, but they can take full sun in cooler climates. Violets prefer rich, moist soil with good drainage. Divide plants or detach runners each year to avoid overcrowding and to promote spring flowering. For heaviest bloom fertilize in early spring just before flowering.

How to Harvest and Store—The leaves should be picked when tender and can be used fresh or dried. The flowers can also be dried and are picked any time the plant is blooming.

How to Use—Flowers and leaves can be used to make a soothing tea, or to add color to jellies, punches, wines and salads. Oils extracted from the flowers are used in perfumes. Decoratively, the flowers can be dried, pressed and used in floral arrangements.

Artemisia absinthium

WORMWOOD, COMMON

Ornamental, cosmetic, tea

There are several species of wormwood, but none is as common as *Artemisia absinthium,* or as it is aptly called, common wormwood. Known for its bitterness, historically it has been used to rid people of internal worms, repel insects, disinfect hospitals, cure indigestion and restore appetites. It was also thought to fight off the effects of certain poisons. Commercially, it's used in perfumes, absinthe, beers and vermouth. It has been placed around clothes to protect them from insects.

Wormwood: from the nursery, after six weeks, harvested leaves.

Roman wormwood: from the nursery, after six weeks.

Old woman wormwood

Fernleaf yarrow

It is an exceptionally attractive landscape plant, either in a gray garden or as a background for a perennial border. Native to parts of Europe, it has adapted to areas of the United States and Canada. It is a wide-spreading woody perennial that can reach 5 feet high. Its leaves are silvery gray, finely divided and fuzzy. They have a bitter taste and musty aroma. Inconspicuous yellow flowers appear from midsummer to fall.

'Lambrook Silver' is an especially attractive variety with a richer silver color and a lower growth habit than common wormwood.

Roman wormwood, *A. pontica*, is heavily branched and 2 to 4 feet tall. It has small, silvery leaves and drooping white flowers. It is used in sachets and vermouth.

Old women wormwood, beach wormwood or dusty miller, *A. stellerana*, has a creeping habit and grows 24 to 30 inches high. Its soft, textured leaves are whiter than common wormwood and have a felt-like texture. Fast growing and dense, it produces spike-like clusters of very attractive yellow flowers and is handsome in the garden. It is used commercially to fatten livestock.

Fringed wormwood, *A. frigida*, grows 16 inches or less, forming a mat with finely cut, silvery white leaves. Excellent in the landscape.

How to Grow—Grow from divisions taken in spring or fall. It roots easily from cuttings. Seeds germinate slowly. Prefers full sun or light shade and well-drained soil, slightly on the clay side. Can tolerate poor soil and drought. Roots deeply, so prepare soil accordingly.

All wormwoods should be trimmed in spring or they become leggy. Divide and replant every two or three years to keep them growing vigorously.

How to Harvest and Store—Harvest leaves any time and use either fresh or dried.

How to Use—Wormwoods are excellent landscape plants, adding interesting color and texture to the garden. It is said that a weak wormwood tea stimulates the appetite.

Achillea millefolium

YARROW
Ornamental, medicinal, dye

Remove flowers and stalks to the base when they fade.

This tough, weedy plant often thrives in vacant city lots. It also makes an outstanding border or specimen plant in a home garden. Dark green or silver foliage contributes an unusual texture and color. Common and woolly yarrow can be mowed to make useful ground covers.

Yarrow is sometimes called *staunchgrass* or *soldier's woundwort*. Both these names and the Greek name for its genus *Achillea,* may come from the legend that Achilles used yarrow to stanch the blood and heal the wounds of his soldiers during the Trojan war. In the 16th century it was believed that inhaling powdered yarrow would cause the nose to bleed and therefore relieve a headache. This gives yarrow another common name, nosebleed.

Several species and varieties are generally available:

Common yarrow, *A. millefolium,* grows to about 3 feet and has grayish green leaves. Flowers are usually white, but there are varieties with reddish flowers. 'Rosea' has pink, 'Fire King' has dark red and 'Cerise Queen' has bright red flowers.

Fernleaf yarrow, *A. filipendulina,* is the most common. You have probably seen it dried in florists' shops. It grows to 5 feet high with dark green, finely divided, almost fern-like leaves. It has tiny, bright yellow, daisy-like flowers compressed in a large, flat-topped cluster. 'Gold Plate' has flowers 5 to 6 inches wide. 'Coronation' grows only 3 feet high, but has flowers just as bright, bold and wide. Both are breathtaking in a perennial border teamed with ornamental onions, agapanthus, royal blue delphiniums or red-hot poker plants.

Silver yarrow, *A. clavennae* or *A. argentea,* has extremely attractive, silvery gray, unserrated leaves and white flowers. It grows to about 1 foot.

Woolly yarrow, *A. tomentosa,* is low growing, with deep green, fuzzy, finely divided leaves. In midsummer, flower stalks carrying bright yellow flowers reach about 6 inches high. 'Primrose Beauty' has pale yellow flowers; 'King George', cream-colored ones. Both make excellent spreading ground covers. It is best to mow when flowers begin to fade.

How to Grow—Yarrows are drought tolerant and disease resistant. Given a fair chance, they will thrive in almost any situation. Their only real requirement is good exposure to the sun; shade weakens them. Start from seeds, root divisions made in spring or fall or nursery plants.

To encourage recurrent bloom, remove flowers and stalks to their base as soon as they begin to fade. Some gardeners recommend dividing the clumps every two or three years.

How to Harvest and Store—If grown for dried flowers, cut while in full bloom in late spring or fall. Make bundles and hang them upside down in an airy spot until thoroughly dry. Harvest leaves at flowering. Dry on trays or in bundles.

How to Use—All the yarrows are beautiful in dried arrangements. Dried and powdered tea of common yarrow is said to be good for the digestion. Its flowers produce a yellow dye when fixed with alum. Fernleaf yarrow makes beautiful indoor arrangements, fresh or dry.

Woolly yarrow

White and Greek yarrow

Pink yarrow

Herbs are Useful

Every good housewife of the 17th century knew how to use her garden plants and considered her herbs especially valuable. She had a separate room—the "stillroom"—where she prepared many products for household use. As you might expect, many of these were culinary, but she also made the family's medicines, household deodorants and her personal cosmetic aids.

Culinary herbs were probably the first ones used by man. It is easy to imagine the discovery of a specific herb's effect on a particular food. Near some prehistoric cave, a plant is thrown onto the fire to keep it going and it immediately releases a wonderful aroma. Soon a little of the same plant is tried in the pot, and eventually a taste is formed for the combination.

Seasoning with herbs is mostly a matter of personal taste, but one principle is to use them carefully at first, testing the food by tasting it. Herbs are to *enhance,* not dominate foods.

Until the advent of modern aspirin and antihistamines, herbs or *botanicals* as they became known, were man's only source of medicines. For many minor ailments today, a cup of herb tea is soothing.

Smell is one of man's most compelling senses and combined with color it creates a link with nature. Potpourri—a mixture of aromatic spices, flowers, leaves and oils—is a wonderful sensory indulgence. Sachets, pomanders and lavender sticks are attractive variations of the same theme.

Commercially prepared face masks, body washes and shampoos that lack harsh ingredients or preservatives are expensive. Beginning on page 150 is a sampling of what you can make at home with herbs from your own garden.

Today, gardeners are rediscovering the rewards of this "stillroom philosophy." Their herbs are a crop to be harvested and channeled into further use. Special satisfaction comes when they bypass expensive, mass-produced commercial products.

You can make your own seasonings, beverages, home remedies for minor ailments, gifts, decorations, tints and dyes, and cosmetics of all kinds.

Here we present an selection of herbal do-it-yourself-and-be-proud projects. This advice comes from modern home economists, herbalists and from people who have shared old "recipes."

The violets at the rear of this photo contribute their flowery essence to the candies, jellies, candles, potpourri and fragrance in the foreground.

Harvesting Herbs

One of the delights of herb gardening comes at harvest time. But for most herbs, you do not have to wait for the perfect moment. You can harvest the fresh leaves of many culinary herbs at any time during the growing season. Do not cut off too many at once or further growth will be hindered. Though any healthy leaves can be used, pick the most tender, young growing tips first. Nipping these has the added benefit of stimulating bushy growth. Basil, chives, mint, marjoram, rosemary, parsley, sage and thyme will provide fresh leaves all season.

The time to harvest is when the herb's oil content is at maximum. For most leafy herbs, this is when the flower buds are just beginning to open. The mints are an exception. They are at their peak when in full flower. Seeds are harvested after their color changes from green to brown, but before they drop. Harvest roots in the fall, at the end of the growing season, when they are fully developed and storing as much food as possible. Harvest herb flowers, such as chamomile, when they reach full flower.

The best time to cut herbs is on a dry, sunny morning after the dew has dried, but before the sun dissipates the volatile oils. Remove seedheads and flowers just below the blossom. Cut leafy herbs about halfway down the stem, leaving enough stem for a second growth. In the fall, cut annual herbs to the ground and perennial herbs about halfway.

Storing Herbs

You can preserve herbs between layers of salt or in olive oil. But the most convenient methods today are drying and freezing.

Drying—Even in mild climates, herb quality and quantity will be less in winter than summer. The best way to have the flower and fragrance of herbs during the winter months is to dry them. Some herbs, such as sage, rosemary, bay, spearmint, lovage, thyme, marjoram and oregano, dry very well and retain their full flavor. In fact, some cooks prefer dried oregano to fresh. Home-dried herbs will be of much higher quality than commercial ones. There are two main methods of drying herbs. The first is the traditional way of hanging the herbs in bunches to dry. This works best with long-stemmed, leafy herbs. Rinse the cut stems gently in cool water to remove dirt. Shake off excess water. Remove dead or discolored leaves. Gather the stems into small bundles and tie their ends together with string. Keep the various herbs separate and label each kind. Hang the bunches upside down in a warm, well-ventilated location. An attic, basement, spare room, or an enclosed porch make good drying places. Do not dry herbs in direct sun because this will spoil their color and dissipate their oils. When the herbs are thoroughly dry and brittle, take down the bundles and strip the leaves off the stems.

Another practical method of drying herbs, especially short-stemmed herbs and flowers, requires a drying screen. You can use ordinary window screens laid flat on bricks or blocks so they are off the ground, or you can construct your own screens using 1x2 boards and window screen. Good air circulation is what you are after, so pick a spot either indoors or out that is warm, well-ventilated and out of direct sun.

For most leafy herbs, all you do is strip the fresh leaves from the stem and spread them on the screen. For herbs with very small leaves, such as the thymes, it is easier to spread the whole herb on the screen rather than stripping off the tiny leaves. Turn the drying leaves periodically so that each leaf is fully exposed to the air and dries completely. They should be dry in about 7 to 10 days, but this will vary with weather and the kind of herb.

Seedheads and flowers of anise, caraway, coriander and dill are dried in essentially the same manner as leaves, but the dried seeds must be separated from the chaff. Place the dried seedhead in a pie tin or similar shallow container and gently blow over it while shaking the pan. The lighter chaff will readily blow out. Shake seeds that are still enclosed within the seed capsule to release them, or roll them between your hands. Once the seeds are clean of chaff, dry them for another 7 to 10 days before storing them.

Dried and cleaned seed can be used for culinary purposes or stored for planting next spring. You can protect seed stored for culinary use from pests by *blanching*. Just dip the seedheads into boiling water before drying. However, blanched seeds will not germinate and are useless for planting.

It is also easy and considerably quicker to dry herbs in a microwave oven. Spread one layer of herbs over a paper towel on the bottom of the oven. Lay another paper towel on top. Run the oven on low for about 2 minutes. If the herbs are not fully dry in that time, turn them over and set the machine for another 1 or 2 minutes. Thick-leaved herbs with lots of moisture, such as basil and comfrey, should be dried in the air for about 3 days before you put them in a microwave oven.

Once dry, herbs should be stored in air-tight containers in a cool, dry location. Decorative or functional

Right: Herbs being dried on rack and drying screen; basket of dried lavender leaves; roses being preserved by use of silica gel.

Separate dried herb leaves from stems before using.

Season to Taste

Almost every American cook who has prepared a meal for an important guest, looking up special recipes, buying ingredients, including at least one herb—has had this happen: The guest eats with gusto and compliments her lavishly on being a "gourmet" cook, only to finally say, "Well, as for me, I don't go in for this gourmet business. I believe in good old-fashioned cooking."

Smile at the irony: The same person who thinks that it is vaguely suspect when *you* cook chicken with fennel or rice with oregano, probably feels that it is virtuous and patriotic when *she* bakes gingerbread or pickles cucumbers.

In both cases, of course, it is herb cookery: combining good foods with good seasonings for contrast and compatibility. In neither case can Americans take credit beyond knowing a good thing when they see it.

It's not that herb cookery has no history in the U.S.A. Early cookbooks and diaries include many herbs in recipes for such things as hangtown fry, hoe cakes, hush puppies, jerky, shoofly pie, chess pie and apple pandowdy—even for succotash, a corn-and-bean recipe borrowed from the Indians. But most food and herb associations, such as dill with pickles, ginger in cake or oregano with pizza, are intentional transplants from one "old country" or another. In fact, Americans have almost no formalized national ritual of pairing certain foods with certain herbs.

As a consequence there is a certain national shyness—almost suspicion—about herb cookery, even though a revolution has taken place in our openness to foods and flavors. Before World War II, "seasoning" was salt, pepper and butter. Rosemary was for remembrance, mint was for jelly, and anyone daring enough to pronounce "oregano" did so with "Oregon" as its root. Today herbs are a multimillion dollar industry. Supermarkets give the pretty jars a special section, and architects specify custom-built herb shelves for kitchens.

Yet thousands of American cooks use savory, as an example, only when a recipe specifies it, or coriander only if they are producing a Mexican meal for guests.

Unwittingly, the herb industry itself and well-meaning cookbook writers might have done herbs a disservice. One of the least rewarding places to look for guidance is on the label of an herb jar or in a cookbook chart. "Good with poultry, fish and vegetables," or "Use with green beans, cabbage and Brussels sprouts," are meant to be encouraging, but instead they are ominous. To the willing but unsure cook, the implication is obvious: What works with poultry, fish and

glass, metal and ceramic containers are good for storing herbs. Don't use paper or cardboard containers because they absorb the herb's oils. Keep glass jars out of the sun to avoid bleaching.

Check the stored herbs the first week or two to be sure no moisture is collecting on the inside of the container. Moisture indicates that the herbs are not thoroughly dry and can cause mold and destroy the herbs. Remove and dry the herbs for a few more days.

Freezing—Many leafy herbs such as mint, French tarragon and sweet marjoram can be either dried or frozen. Herbs such as basil, fennel, dill, parsley, chervil, chives and burnet do not dry well, but freeze perfectly.

Harvest and wash the herbs just as you would for drying. Then gently pat them dry, remove the leaves from their stems and place them in a small plastic sandwich bag or plastic freezer box. If you use plastic bags, press out all excess air before sealing. Store each herb in a separately labeled package, or make up packets of your favorite herb blends.

Salting—Salting is simple and probably one of the oldest methods of preserving herbs. Simply alternate layers of salt and herbs in a covered crock or jar. Middle layers of salt should just cover herbs; the first and last salt layers should be slightly thicker. Kosher salt is usually preferred. Basil and tarragon are two of the best herbs to preserve this way.

Salting herbs not only preserves them for future use, but the salt takes on the herb flavor as well. See page 137.

vegetables would ruin a perfectly good pot roast. What is recommended for cabbage probably won't work with carrots.

Furthermore, few food writers can resist admonishing the reader to use herbs "sparingly." It is almost as if they visualized cooks upending their herb jars into dinner, so often do they temper their recommendations and enthusiasms with this prim reminder. The result is that all over America cooks carefully halve 1/4 teaspoon with a knife and live with the same jar of spice for years. Using old herbs sparingly is almost the same as not using them at all.

These writers do mean well, however, and are urging you to use herbs judiciously and thoughtfully. Sample different herbs to learn their flavors, analyzing each for its particular charm. Consider what you want each to do in every dish, and taste as you cook.

The writers also mean you should use herbs discreetly, with knowledge. Recall all you have learned about them from recipes you have read and foreign foods you have eaten. Good herb cooks use herbs as *seasonings,* not *ingredients,* and you should do the same.

International cookbooks are the best teachers you can find, because traditional dishes are the result of years of using the materials at hand. You will discover that through the ages herbs have found natural companions—other herbs, other foods, in other cultures.

More important, you will learn that these natural companions are not a matter of chemical affinity, but are the simple result of expediency: They were available.

Thus, other peoples' food patterns become a door-opener, not a door-closer. When a French cook ties a selection of herbs into a tidy little bundle, and when a Chinese cook slices ginger into the stir-fry oil, and when a farm cook sprinkles borage on the soup, they are using herbs as seasonings, just as they do salt and pepper.

Just as you salt to taste, use your own judgment when it comes to herbs. There is no exact rule for the correct amount to use. The pungency of each herb differs, and its effect on different food varies. With dried herbs, age also affects flavor.

FLAVORS OF THE WORLD

One of the blessings of the burgeoning herb industry is that we can now buy bottled herbal blends such as curry powder, chili powder, *bouquet garni, fines herbes,* and Chinese five-spice powder. These commercial mixes are tasty and convenient, but don't believe that they are the last word, or even orthodox, especially if that closes the door on your own herb adventuring.

Curry powder—In India, a cook buys fresh and dried herbs at stalls in the town market and grinds and mixes them daily. She is likely to choose from ginger, cardamom, cayenne, turmeric and cumin, but there is no specific formula. It depends on the menu, the guests and what is available.

Commercial curry powders vary. They usually contain six or more of the following herbs: coriander, cumin, fenugreek, turmeric, ginger, pepper, mace, cardamom and cloves. To make your own, start with a simple curry base using equal proportions of coriander seeds, cardamom seeds and dried ginger. Add at least as much turmeric and some cayenne. Be careful, though. Cayenne is very strong. Of course you may vary ingredients considerably. Cumin, mustard and dry chili powder are often added.

Strip flavorful leaves by pulling fingers along stem.

Finely chopped chives are a delightful and attractive addition sprinkled on top an omelet or mixed into a salad.

You might not want to make your own curry powder from scratch, but you should always feel free to improve on a prepared mix by adding herbs. And you will get closer to an authentic curried dish if you always do what the Indian cook does: sauté the blend before stirring it into the sauce.

Chili powder—Historical credit for combining such herbs as oregano, cumin and hot red peppers goes to the Aztecs, but it took a Texan in the early 19th century to put that mix of spices together in a powder. Legend has it that he was trying to recreate a curried dish he had tasted in India.

Mexican cooks, who never use anything called chili powder, develop the flavor from ingredients on hand. Chilies, oregano and cumin are essential, with proportions varying according to personal tastes and particular foods. Commercial chili powders consist of cumin, garlic, coriander, oregano and several varieties of chili pods, principally the *ancho* from Mexico and the *hontaka* from Japan. You can make your own mix by grinding five to seven dried chilies into powder and adding teaspoon amounts of the other herbs of your choice to start. Then add garlic, coriander and onion as your taste dictates.

Bouquet garni and *fines herbes*—As herb blends, these are misleading. To the French cook, *bouquet garni* (bo·kay gar·ne) and *fines herbes* (feen herbs) are methods, not formulas. For a recipe that calls for a *bouquet garni*, she ties fresh herbs into cheesecloth and drops it into the simmering dish. In dishes described as *fines herbes,* she chops herbs finely to stir in or sprinkle on top. The difference is a nicety that, to accomplished French cooks, is so automatic that they no longer talk about it. *Bouquet garni* is used in foods that are simmered so long that the flavor goes out of the herbs and into the pot; the tidy wrap means that it can be quickly retrieved and discarded. *Fines herbes* is used in cold foods like salads, quick-cooking foods like omelets and fish, or on top of anything that needs a color or flavor lift.

Bouquet garni, in classical French cooking, combines parsley, marjoram, thyme and bay leaf, with proportions adjusted to the dish. In everyday practice, the French cook uses other aromatic herbs—basil, chervil, tarragon, burnet—according to personal preferences and the companion foods. Lemon thyme is a favorite with fish dishes; dried fennel is added to soups, stews, poultry and turkey gravies. Commercial blends usually include basil, summer savory, marjoram, oregano, rosemary, sage, dill, thyme and tarragon.

To the traditional French cook, *fines herbes* are simply fresh parsley; to the Italian it means specifically flat leaf parsley. Both parsleys are finely chopped. But here again the cook uses her own discretion. In many American cookbooks it has come to mean a chopped mixture of parsley, tarragon, chives and chervil. One of the major commercial mixes includes thyme, oregano, sage, rosemary, marjoram and basil. If you make your own, vary the mixture to suit the food. Marjoram

Bouquet garni is a method of seasoning long-simmering foods. Wrapped in small bags, the herbs are easily removed from the pot. Specific herbs used can vary but usually include parsley, marjoram, thyme and a bay leaf.

Making a *bouquet garni* with fresh herbs is as simple as tying the stems together to make a bunch.

is excellent in a chicken broth or with any poultry. Add savory to a bean soup or basil to tomato dishes. Italian cooks always put a few sprigs of rosemary on a roasting leg of lamb. The flavor permeates both the lamb and the kitchen.

Chinese five-spice powder—Also known as *five heavenly spices,* this is a finely ground powder that lends the distinctive Oriental fragrance and pungence to marinades and sauces and to "red-cooked" meat and poultry.

There are many possible variations of the recipe, but most specify a finely ground mixture of these five spices in these approximate amounts: 1 tablespoon cinnamon, 1/2 teaspoon cloves, 1 tablespoon Szechuan peppercorns, 1 tablespoon fennel seeds and 6 whole star anise seeds, ground.

Grind each ingredient individually, measure and mix together, then grind the mixture. This will make a bit more than 3 tablespoons, which is plenty for most recipes. Store leftover spice in an airtight jar.

Szechuan pepper (*Zanthoxylum piperitum*) is similar to our black pepper, but has a somewhat delayed and more intense flavor. It is essential to Szechuan-style Chinese cooking, but black pepper can be substituted in five-spice powder.

HANDY HERBAL BLENDS

Make these when you have the time and inclination, in quantities that will last for six months to a year. Store them in airtight containers away from strong sunlight and heat, but in a spot near enough the stove to make use convenient. Of course you should vary the recipes to suit your own tastes. All of these blends can also be wrapped and used for gifts.

For poultry stuffing or chicken soup

3 tablespoons sage	1 tablespoon lovage
1 tablespoon lemon thyme	1 tablespoon parsley
2 tablespoons marjoram	

For soups and stews

1 tablespoon savory	1-1/2 teaspoons rosemary
2 tablespoons marjoram	1 tablespoon lovage

For tomato sauce

2 tablespoons basil	1-1/2 teaspoons oregano
1 tablespoon marjoram	1 tablespoon parsley

Salad herbs

1 tablespoon basil	1 tablespoon tarragon
1 tablespoon parsley	1-1/2 teaspoons thyme

Fish herbs

1 tablespoon basil	1-1/2 teaspoons dill or
1 tablespoon parsley	tarragon or fennel
	1 whole bay leaf

Herbs aromatique

This recipe makes about 2-1/2 cups and is a great convenience to have on hand. Use it with hamburger, broiled chicken, baked potatoes and many other foods.

2 cups coarse (Kosher) salt
1 large bulb of garlic; peel cloves and cut in half
2 tablespoons ground white pepper
1 tablespoon ground ginger
1-1/2 tablespoons poultry stuffing seasoning
   (see recipe in previous column)
3 tablespoons paprika, Hungarian if possible
1 tablespoon dry mustard
3 tablespoons chili powder
1 tablespoon celery seed
1 tablespoon onion powder
1 tablespoon dried dill
1 tablespoon fresh oregano or basil (optional)

Mix all ingredients in a blender or food processor. If you use a blender, use a carrot or celery stalk to push the garlic into the blades.

Cooking with Herbs

• When you are experimenting with an herb, remember it is far easier to add more than take out.

• Herb blends should be subtle. Use one strongly flavored herb as a basic flavor, and add other herbs to complement it. Use different herb blends for different foods.

• Basil, rosemary, oregano, thyme, sage and tarragon are dominate herbs. As a rule, they do not mix well with each other.

• The amount of seasoning to use in a recipe will vary with the freshness of the herb. Fresh or recently dried herbs have the strongest flavor.

• Reduce the amount of herb used by 2/3 to 3/4 when substituting dried herbs for fresh.

• Revive the flavor of dried herbs by soaking them in 1 teaspoon lemon juice for about 10 minutes.

• Sauté herbs in butter or oil, heating the mixture gently, to draw out the flavor. Refrigerate unused portions.

• Use about 1/4 teaspoon (a *pinch*) of dried herbs or 1 teaspoon fresh herbs to 4 servings of food, 1 pound of meat or 1 pint of sauce.

• Add herbs at the same time as salt and pepper. Avoid cooking herbs too long in foods such as stews. Add herbs during the last half hour of cooking. Some herbs become bitter if overcooked.

• Add herbs to juices or cold sauces and butters well ahead of time or let them stand together overnight.

• Before adding the measured amount of an herb to a recipe, crush it in the palm of one hand with the heel of the other. This will release the full flavor.

Kitchen Herbs

Cooking with herbs is both fun and challenging. Don't be timid—learn to use herbs with appreciation, conviction and good taste.

Using the theory that people who grow herbs in their gardens are likely to be excellent sources of herb knowledge, we sought out members of herb societies and other experienced herb gardeners, cooks, home economists and food writers from across the United States. We accumulated their opinions and advice, along with guidance from experts and books on herb cooking of other lands. Here is what we've learned.

ANISE

These pungent, licorice-flavored seeds have a time-honored place in baked goods, and many cooks never go beyond stirring anise into cakes, cookies, bread or coffee cake. But Croatian cooks stir it into sautéing liver, and Indians simmer it in generous quantities with tomatoes and serve the mix as a relish. It is a traditional ingredient in German *pfefferneuse* and in some regional Spanish Easter cakes. The English like it in rum sauce over puddings. Early American cookbooks mention anise sugar, which was sprinkled on hot cakes and possibly used on hot buttered bread, like cinnamon toast.

One cook tells us, "When my Swedish mama used anise in cooked icings, she soaked the seeds in hot water for an hour or so, then drank the water as she stirred in the seeds."

Sweet liqueurs, such as anisette, are flavored with anise seed. They can be used in cooking when you want the flavor of anise, but do not want your dishes to contain the anise seeds. They can be used in recipes for soups, creamy dressings and for basting meat.

When considering how to use anise, remember that its flavor is similar to fennel. It can usually be used wherever fennel is used. Because it is a seed, it can be a refreshing substitute for caraway, cumin, sesame, poppy, celery or any other cooking seed. In baking, try anise wherever you use cinnamon, nutmeg, cloves or allspice. It is good in French dressing, in pickle-and-egg sandwiches or goulash.

If you grow anise, try using the leaves in cooking. They are less robust and less aromatic than seeds, but more decorative. Try them with sweet fruits, carrots, parsnips and yams.

Lemon thyme, being cut here, is a kitchen herb worth investigating.

BASIL

Many cooks feel that basil is the most important of all herbs.

Basil is a traditional and delicious ingredient in such Italian favorites as lasagna, spaghetti and pizza, or in any dish that uses tomatoes.

But that is only the beginning. Basil sharpens the flavor of any vegetable, brightens any salad, including fruit salads. It enriches the flavors of mushrooms, fish, cottage or cream cheese, white sauce and even oatmeal.

Interestingly, early American cookbooks mention basil most often as an ingredient in baking, particularly in fruit pies, upside-down cakes and baked fruits.

Pesto—*Pesto* sauce is used on many Italian dishes. There are probably as many recipes for pesto as there are cooks who love basil.

In a blender mix 1 cup basil leaves, 1/3 cup parsley, 1 cup grated Parmesan cheese, and 6 tablespoons olive oil. Use it as a sauce for pasta or vegetables.

Pesto enthusiasts have been known to steam basil as a vegetable and serve it with butter, salt, pepper and a garnish of chopped tomatoes.

"Dried basil is not nearly as flavorful as fresh, so shake the jar hard," an Italian neighbor advises.

Fresh basil can be preserved in salt. Simply place leaves between layers of salt, as described on page 122. Don't freeze basil, just refrigerate it. Basil does not look good as a garnish because the leaves darken and go limp.

BAY LAUREL

This herb is a must in *bouquet garni,* a tradition in *bouillabaisse* and spaghetti. Bay laurel is pungent enough to stand up to strong-flavored beef, lamb, liver and ham. Scandinavians add it with whole cloves to the cooking water for tongue. Turks alternate bay leaves with fish on skewers, then broil it kebab-style over hot coals. It is used almost everywhere to flavor soups.

Probably the best cooking guideline you can have is: If it simmers, it can take a bay leaf. Remove the leaf before serving, because it is unpalatable.

Bay leaves imported into the United States are milder than California ones. But the European bay is easily grown and obtainable from most nurseries.

BORAGE

This was a favorite of American pioneers and is highly respected in Europe as an herb that goes well with cheese. It has a slightly bitter, cucumber-like flavor.

Small plants and young leaves on older plants are excellent when cooked as greens. The bristly hairs disappear in cooking. You can also chop leaves and use

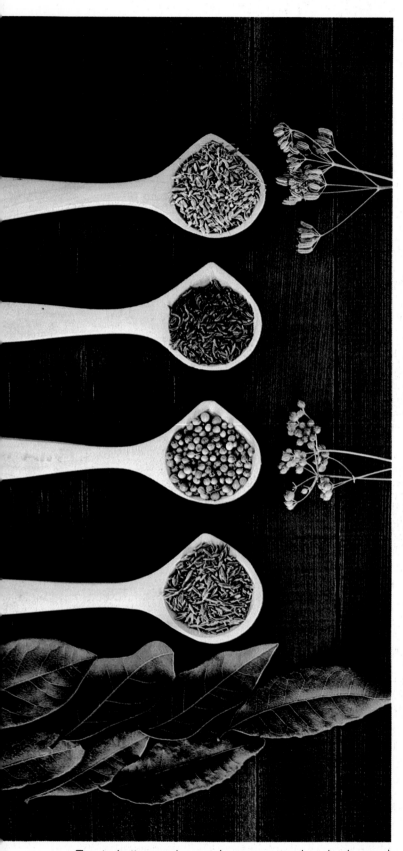

Top to bottom: anise seed; caraway seed; coriander seed; cumin seed; dried bay leaves.

them as you would any herb for a garnish. Mix borage leaves with sour cream and mayonnaise for a delicious summer sandwich.

You can eat the large stalk raw as you would cucumber, or in chunks in salad.

The blue flowers can be used in fruit drinks or scattered over a platter of sliced tomatoes in vinaigrette.

Directions for using borage blossoms for cake or cookie decorations are on page 141. Fresh blossoms also yield a mildly spicy tea, described on page 143.

CARAWAY

Similar in flavor to cumin, caraway is a traditional ingredient in Danish cheese, German cabbage and sauerkraut, and in rye bread. It is the chief flavoring ingredient for pumpernickel bread, which was invented by and named for a 15th-century Swiss baker named Pumper Nickel.

Scandinavians cook it with fish, Italians with chestnuts, the Irish with potatoes, especially potato pancakes, and the Dutch in waffles. In India, it is sprinkled on hot, thin French fries to serve with tea. Country cooks stir caraway into pickling brine for beets, and others like it with sage, on noodles or in creamed tuna.

Caraway is compatible with oranges, melon and apples. Try adding it to apple pie or applesauce, or lightly dip apple slices in crushed caraway seeds. French toast with orange marmalade, a dollop of sour cream and a sprinkling of caraway can be a delicious breakfast or dessert. A compote of caraway, honeydew melon and grapes with maybe a dash of kummel could upstage a pumpkin pie. A roll of ham, casaba melon and caraway makes an elegant hors d'oeuvre or first course.

Once you have caraway in your garden, you can also experiment with other parts of the plant. Add chopped leaves to stews, stuffings, meat loaf, anything that strikes you as dull. Pare and cook the roots as you would parsnips, or grind them and use as you would the seed.

CHERVIL

Fresh chervil is best. In cooking, the flavor dissipates quickly, so it is best to add chervil just before serving.

It is sometimes called *gourmet parsley*—not because it is fancier but because French cooks love it. It enhances the flavors of other herbs. With just a whisper of licorice flavor, it is sweeter and milder than parsley.

For some reason, chervil seems especially compatible with white or light-colored foods. Try it with cream soups and chowders, corn and corn puddings, potato dumplings and potato salads. Its delicately piquant flavor mixes well with fish and seafood, and in some parts of Europe it is served with oysters.

Norwegians use it in their beloved *gurkas dilisas*, which are cucumbers scooped out and stuffed with a mixture of cream cheese, anchovies, dill, green onions and chervil.

Hungarians use chervil generously in mushroom soup. French country cooks make a soup from potatoes and chopped chervil cooked in chicken stock, laced with vinegar and lemon.

You might want to try this salad dressing on fruit salad. It should be made several hours ahead. Combine 1/2 cup each oil and white wine vinegar. Add 1 tablespoon sugar, 1/2 teaspoon nutmeg, a few drops of lemon juice and 2 or 3 branches chervil, chopped fine. Shake or stir to dissolve the sugar, and serve.

CHIVES

Chives lend a subtle onion flavor to any recipe that suggests a touch of onion. They are favored with cream cheese or cottage cheese. Chives may be used to flavor an omelet or butter, and, of course, they are great on baked potatoes. See *fines herbes*, page 124.

CORIANDER

Called *cilantro* by the Mexicans and marketed as Chinese parsley in the United States, it is a staple in Mexican and Chinese cooking. Other cultures value it, too. It is an ingredient in curry powder and widely used in India. Pakistanis use crushed seeds in basting or marinating fish, and in ground meat. Moroccans use it with ginger and cumin on kebabs. Panamanians like it in a lime-spiked stew of mixed meats, squash and green bananas. Portuguese add chopped fresh leaves to two national favorites: *acorda*, bread softened with the boiling stock of the catch of the day, and *bolinhos de bacalhau*, codfish cakes. Palestinians serve fresh fava beans dusted with chopped cilantro leaves and garlic.

You won't go wrong by adding coriander—either as a seasoning or leafy garnish—to any Mexican food, including *guacamole*, an avocado dip, and refried beans. A *little* sautéed with butter, lemon juice and garlic is delicious over prawns.

The flavor of ground seeds is strong and has been likened to oranges, lemons, sage and caraway. Early American cooks used the seeds in pastries, baked food and pickling brines. They are also used commercially in sausage and gin.

A home economist writes, "Food writers lately have been saying it is the Chinese substitute for parsley. It is not. The Chinese use parsley, too, and they like it well enough to not *want* a substitute for it. They use neither parsley nor coriander for quick color garnish, and they use coriander—in many, many dishes—in very prescribed ways, for the particular quality it brings to other foods and seasonings."

Stir it into any wok combination, or sprinkle it on top afterwards. Or use the chopped leaves as a curry condiment to reinforce the curry flavor.

CUMIN

The Romans used ground cumin seed as a substitute for pepper. It is a quick way to liven bland foods like noodles, rice and potatoes. It is also nice on baked carrots and interesting in marinades and basting sauce for pork.

The Belgians use it with pot roast, the Dutch in *hotspot*, potatoes mashed with carrots and parsnips. The Austrians use it in potato dumplings, the Hebrews in unleavened bread, the Indonesians with spareribs and *saté*, and the Turks add it to pilaf. The Portuguese use it with codfish and in cakes. Latin Americans mix it in corn-tomato-zucchini medleys, the Armenians in lamb stew, and the Scandinavians in cookies. In Valencia, the traditional *cocido*, a three-course stew of meat, vegetables and beans, is accompanied by a bowl of cumin. Likewise, Moroccan *mechoui*, roasted lamb, is served with bowls of cumin and salt for dipping.

Cumin is an ingredient of curry powder, and Indians use it alone stirred into yogurt as a relish. It's also an ingredient in commercial chili powder. Mexicans and Central Americans use it in enchiladas, tamales, skillet dishes, and *huevos rancheros*, an egg dish, among other things.

The fact that the Swiss use it to flavor cheese may inspire you to try it in any mild, cheese dish. Cheese fondue with cumin is a near-classic.

Though it isn't technically a substitute for caraway, it is likely to be good in anything caraway is good in.

DILL

Dill is a standby for pickles, but good cooks reach for dill seeds and leaves for a wide range of other foods, too. The leaf is sharply delicate. The seed is slightly bitter.

Sprinkle the leaves on salads, vegetables, fish and sauces. Use the seeds in long-simmered stews and soups. It is especially beloved in Scandinavia, where it grows wild. The Finns make a memorable buttermilk-dill soup. The Danes use it for garnish on almost any open-faced sandwich, and the Swedes and Norwegians make a famous "dilly bread." Dill is also used in cream sauce for their Christmas *lutefisk*. In the United States, dilled green beans, dilled carrots and dilled new potatoes are spring favorites and are highly compatible with Easter ham. All can be made with either leaves or seeds.

Top to bottom: dill seed and dried, crushed dill leaves; fennel seed; ginger, fresh and dried; garlic.

Mixed with cream cheese or sour cream, dill makes a delicious dip that is especially tasty with asparagus. Mixed into sour cream, it is a good topping for baked potatoes. Dill tastes great with cucumbers, even out of the pickle jar.

FENNEL

To Italian cooks, fennel is one of the essentials. They value its delicate anise-like flavor and use it in pasta, salad and breads.

All parts of the plant are edible. Sprinkle crushed seeds over crumb-topped casseroles, or stir them into the dipping crumbs for fish or veal, or rub them into pork roast before baking.

Fennel leaves and fish are superb together. Add them to basting sauce when broiling, to the water when poaching, or to melted butter to pour over. Or, for a memorable meal, place dried stalks on top of the coals when barbecuing.

The stalks can be prepared any way appropriate to celery. Eat them raw, simmer in water or bouillion, or braise with garlic in oil. Add stalks to soups or stews; do it towards the last because it cooks as fast as celery.

To make a delicious fennel soup, thinly slice a large root. Simmer it in a quart of chicken stock for about half an hour. Strain, add salt and pepper to taste and garnish with parsley or borage.

FRENCH SORREL

The British have used sorrel since at least 1599, and have lauded it for its healthful qualities. A 16th century cook recommended a soup made from 2 pounds sorrel, 1-1/2 quarts water, 6 tablespoons lemon juice and one egg. It was served cold with a garnish of sour cream and hard boiled eggs.

Today the English cook it with red beans, chop it into omelets, purée it into sauces for vegetables, cold fish or hard-boiled eggs, and combine it with buttermilk to make a cold soup. The Irish combine it with pickled mushroom, lemon juice and oil to make *Finn Sorrel Salad.* They also use it with beef, vegetables and barley to make *craibechan.* The French make a soup with sorrel called *potage crème d'oseille.*

Sauces flavored with sorrel are good with many kinds of fish, especially oily ones. Some like sorrel chopped into green salads. Labeled a "bitter spinach," sorrel can be used most of the ways as spinach.

GARLIC

Garlic grown in Europe is milder than the variety grown in North America. It is not uncommon to see workmen in Greece eating an entire bulb of garlic with lunch, clove by clove, much as we would eat potato chips. Even so, many European cooks are puzzled by Americans' timidity with garlic, and amused by the almost cultlike custom that grew up in the '50s of rubbing a wooden salad bowl with garlic, then discarding the pulp. "That's like rubbing your shower cap with a dab of shampoo to wash your hair," says a grinning woman from Greece.

There is little point in discussing specific uses of garlic; if you like it, you probably already use garlic salt, garlic powder and cloves. But we can perhaps encourage you to even greater use with these three recipes—all simple, all classics in their homeland and all dependent on heavy use of garlic.

Aioli comes from France; some say it is the best thing that ever happened to cold cooked artichokes, sliced raw mushrooms, raw carrot and celery sticks. Crush 8 to 10 large cloves of garlic and beat into 2 cups commercial or homemade mayonnaise. Serve as a dip.

Cevapcici (pronounced chiv·o·pchee·chee) accounts for the heavenly odors at dinnertime in homes up and down the Dalmatian Coast and throughout Yugoslavia. Crush cloves from entire bulb. Stir into 1-1/2 pounds ground meat—a mixture of twice as much beef as pork is the most nearly authentic. Form into fingers, cook over coals and serve on chopped onion.

Sopa de ajo, garlic soup, is to the Spaniards what tomato soup is to us. Sauté at least 2 tablespoons finely chopped garlic in olive oil, then stir in 3 cups coarse bread crumbs and sauté until the bread turns golden. Pour in 1-1/2 quarts water or chicken stock and simmer uncovered for half an hour. Pulverize the bread with wooden spoon, or stir in a blender. Over low heat, gradually pour in 3 beaten eggs, stirring constantly. Do not boil, but bring to a simmer. Season heavily with salt, cayenne pepper and if you wish, paprika.

If you worry about the lingering odor of garlic after eating, chew on a sprig of fresh parsley.

Some garlic lovers feel so strongly about the superiority of fresh garlic that they dig it up just before they use it. They also enjoy using the delicately flavored stems and flowers. Sprinkling salt on garlic before chopping keeps it from flying around; mashing it with salt mellows the flavor.

GINGER

Much of the joy of herb cookery comes from the respect it gives one for the versatility of cooks around the world. Take ginger, for instance: It is what Orientals season their main dishes with and Americans bake into cookies. It is a far cry from Peking duck to gingersnaps.

Not that baking ginger into dessert is an American phenomenon. Gingerbread is credited to a Rhodes baker of 2400 B.C.

Germans use ginger in *sauerbraten.* Middle Easterners mix it with mustard and garlic as a marinade and cooking sauce for lamb. The Poles use it in stuffed cabbage, Central Americans cook it with sautéed bananas, the Jamaicans in pumpkin soup. The English make it into a sauce or combine it with powdered sugar for use on pudding or fruit; some British cooks consider it a must for plum pudding. Neapolitans use it in their traditional Easter pie, and Jewish people all over the world use it in *tzimmies,* a stew of vegetables and fruits at Rosh Hashanah, and in their Passover cake.

It is an ingredient in our curry powder, and the characteristic seasoning of chutney, a favorite in India for many foods.

Early American cookbooks mention it often, not only for baked desserts but scalloped sweet potatoes, carrot puddings, baked beans and watermelon pickles. Indian pudding, which is basically corn meal and molasses, depends on ginger for its characteristic flavor. In Bayou cookery it is a standby for meat pies and stews.

Try it in the cooking water for artichokes, or stir a bit into rarebit. Some cooks use it in ham glaze, or stir it into commercial vanilla ice cream.

GOOSEFOOT, EPAZOTE

Of the many species of *Chenopodium,* Mexico's *epazote, C. ambrosioides,* is the strongest flavored and most notable. It is a common and essential flavoring of Mayan Indians on Mexico's Yucatan Peninsula. Elsewhere in Mexico, it is used with black beans, corn, mushrooms, fish and shellfish. It is said to reduce gas problems associated with beans. Young plants of this and other *Chenopodium* species are more mild flavored and make a fine tea. Use them in salads, soups and cooked greens.

Note: Eating unusually large amounts of C. ambrosioides may cause dizziness and other more uncomfortable or more serious effects.

HORSERADISH

Horseradish almost always shows up commercially in sauces, such as vinegar, sour cream and mayonnaise. It is too strong to use alone. The sauce dilutes and spreads the flavor. But when you have it in your garden, you can toss it, chopped, into salads. It adds zip to green salads, vegetable salads and rice salads.

You seldom see horseradish served hot or cooked because heat destroys its flavor.

Combined with whipping or sour cream, it is the perfect condiment for pork and tongue, and a traditional one for roast beef and ham. Seafood cocktail sauces would not be the same without it. To make your

Top to bottom: dried lemongrass, dried lemon verbena leaves, dried mint, whole mustard seed, dried and crushed oregano, dried rosemary.

own, stir together catsup, lemon juice and grated horseradish root. You can make a sophisticated thousand island dressing by adding freshly grated horseradish, or give hotdogs new stature by adding it to mustard. It is good in marinades, pickling liquids and salad dressings. Europeans like it grated and mixed with vinegar, and consider it a health-giver, possibly because it *is* rich in vitamin C.

You can stir it into pickle juice after the pickles are gone, and keep it in the refrigerator until some left-over party carrot and celery sticks and cauliflower branches come along. Presto, refrigerator icebox pickles for the next couple of days.

Try this great dip. Mix equal parts liverwurst and sour cream, and add grated horseradish to taste. Add chopped onions for texture.

HYSSOP

This herb is widely used in the Middle East and occasionally by Europeans.

Hyssop is one of the accommodating flavors that goes "sweet" as well as "salty."

Slightly minty, it is good with lamb; Hungarians like it with rabbit. In England, it is traditional with cranberries; they also serve it with stewed or canned fruits, in fruit pies, and in fruit cocktail and fruit drinks. Europeans feel it improves the taste of oily fish and rich meats. A United States gardener likes its nicely bitter contrast to mild summer squashes, and a woman from Australia uses it with sweetbreads and ox tongue.

It is one of the herbs that gets stronger as it cooks, so add it late in the cooking of long-simmering soups and stews.

LEMON BALM

It smells and tastes like lemon, so it is a natural garnish for lemonade, hot or iced tea, fruit cups and fruit salads. It adds piquancy to marinades for poultry or veal and can be rubbed into meat before roasting. It can be used with any fish.

It is delicious with almost any vegetable, especially with beets and spinach.

LEMONGRASS

Leaves and stems are strongly lemon favored and have many kitchen uses, fresh or dry. Use them to flavor wines and teas, soups, curries, sauces and fish. The plant is native in southern Asia and is widely used throughout Asia. To appreciate the culinary virtues of this herb, fry a trout after placing about 6 fresh leaves of lemongrass in its cleaned center cavity.

LEMON VERBENA

Lemon verbena is one of the most strongly aromatic herbs in the garden. For best results in cooking, use fresh leaves. Much of the flavor is lost when they are dried. Use it as a substitute for lemon. It is also good in tea, fruit salad, jams and jellies. It makes a pretty garnish for finger bowls.

Chopped leaves over a green or tomato salad make a pleasant surprise. To make a white sauce for fish, use 2 cups medium white sauce, the juice of 1/2 lemon and 5 or 6 chopped leaves of lemon verbena.

LOVAGE

All parts of this plant are used. Its taste is somewhere between celery and anise. Use the leaves as you would any seasoning herb in salads, vegetable soups and omelets. Cut and blanch the stems and serve as a vegetable, or candy them as you would angelica to garnish cakes. Sprinkle the seeds over meat, bread or cookies. They also make an intriguing herb butter. Grate the roots to make tea or chop them and preserve in honey.

MARJORAM

Marjoram has long been one of the most popular herbs. It was well known to cooks in the Mediterranean areas at least 1,200 years ago, and Renaissance recipes specify it for salads, cheese and egg dishes, with all kinds of fish and meat, and rice. With marjoram you can hardly go wrong.

Along with basil and oregano it is one of the three basic herbs in Italian cooking. People living in the Balkans like it in lentil soup, the Slovenians in dumplings. The Czechs use it in meatballs, the Hungarians in goulash. In England it is traditional with roast goose and chestnut dumplings, and in Ireland with kid.

MINT

Mint made the julep famous. It also sparks up sauces, salad dressings and iced drinks.

It is widely used in Middle Eastern cookery and around the Mediterranean. Syrians and Persians cut it into salads. Greeks stuff it into grape leaves with lamb and rice. Mint-flavored zucchini is a Roman favorite and Morrocans steep it as tea. Fish is often basted or marinated with oregano and mint. The Portuguese like it cooked with fava beans and in their classic *canja*, a soup made from chicken, chicken broth, lemon juice and slightly chopped, fresh mint leaves. The French stir it into chopped onions as a relish, and the English cook it with lentils. In the United States minted apple jelly and lamb go hand in hand. Mint is delicious cooked with cabbage or cauliflower.

MUSTARD

Mustard, ground and mixed into a paste, is widely used as a condiment. See page 92 for an excellent recipe.

OREGANO

As Italian cooks have long known, oregano is delicious with tomatoes and pasta. As Middle Eastern cooks know, it is equally at home with *kasha,* pilaf, legumes, lamb, eggplant and summer squash.

Puerto Ricans use oregano in *sofrito,* a basic cooking sauce for vegetables. Costa Ricans use it in many corn dishes. The Aztecs combined oregano and chili peppers, creating the forerunner of chili powder.

PARSLEY

Many cooks sprinkle it over potatoes, vegetables and soups, primarily for color and eye appeal. But keep in mind its peppery flavor. Use it by the pinch, or the cupful, in paté, dumplings, omelets, court bouillon, marinades and terrines.

Early English cooks made whole plants into parsley pie. In elegant restaurants branches show up deep-fried as a garnish for fried foods. To do this, put branches in a basket and deep fry until crisp. Another standard French method is *en bluches:* pick off leaves, blanch in boiling water, dry well, brown quickly in butter, and pour over cooked vegetables or potatoes, browned butter and all.

In using it as a garnish, you will gain more respect for it if you make the thoughtful distinction between fine and rough chopping, sprigs and branches, depending on the dish.

Don't dry parsley—the flavor disappears.

ROSEMARY

Traditional with pork and veal. If you grow it, try spreading fresh leaves on roasts and poultry before baking.

Rosemary is one of the herbs with a flavor that tastes sweet or salty depending on its use. The British like it in jams, jellies, fruit salad and fruit cups. The Italians use it in tomato sauce, though less lavishly than basil and oregano. Balkan cooks bake it in bread or mix it in butter. Hungarians add it to their vegetable cooking water. It is a favorite of the Spanish, who burn it as incense on certain feast days, and put it into rabbit pie on others. The French stir it into *coq au vin, ragout, vendome sauce* and many other dishes. Middle Easterners and back yard cooks know it is delicious on lamb kebabs.

Top to bottom: dried sage leaves, dried savory leaves, sesame seed, dried tarragon, thyme.

SAGE

This is the herb that perfumes kitchens all over the United States on Thanksgiving—it is traditional in turkey stuffing. It grows in Yugoslavia and Albania and is a favorite seasoning in many native foods. Europeans believe that it helps digest rich foods, which might account for its association with duck and game recipes there.

There are many varieties of sages that can be used to flavor poultry and pork stuffings, sausage, cheese, egg dishes, cooked vegetables and fish. The leaves of clary sage can even be fried like fritters. Pineapple sage finds its way into jams and jellies. See page 98.

Crush or grind leaves to release full flavor. Powdered sage is excellent rubbed on a fresh pork roast before baking. An Italian favorite is made by adding fresh or dried leaves into the frying pan when frying chicken. Sage is a strong-flavored herb, so use it with discretion.

SAVORY

Both summer and winter savory have strong, peppery flavors. Summer savory is usually preferred for cooking because of the texture of its leaf and its milder flavor. The Swiss call it *bohnenkraut,* which means bean herb, either because it is so good with green beans—and in fact any green vegetable—or because they're natural companions in the garden. The Romans used it to flavor vinegar. In the Middle Ages, savory was a favorite seasoning for baked goods.

Like other zesty herbs, savory is equally at home in salads, soups and stews. The English like it with roast duck and game.

SESAME

High in protein, sesame seeds make a good "nut" in many meatless dishes and salads, and on vegetables and breads as well.

Early Romans spread crushed seed on bread, possibly like peanut butter. Iranians grind it into flour and use both seeds and flour in desserts. The Spanish mix it with nuts and honey for a candy-like, unbaked cookie. Chinese make it into oil and use the oil and the seeds in many dishes. Arabs mix sesame seeds or oil with garbanzos to make *tahini.*

Use sesame where you would use almost any other cooking seed: in crumb crusts and toppings, in dipping flour or on casseroles. When you sprinkle seeds on soufflés or over pancakes, they form a crunchy, golden brown crust.

Unless you are pouring sesame seeds on a surface that will be browned in cooking, toast the seeds first to bring out their flavor and crunch.

SHALLOT

Shallots (sha·lots) are among the herbs most used by the French. Their flavor is subtle, a fine blending of onion, garlic and chives. Shallots are specified in many recipes. They are excellent sprinkled on meat and in fish sauces, salad dressing and herbal vinegars.

SWEET CICELY

Every part is edible and has a slight licorice tang. The leaves are sweet enough to substitute for sugar. The green seeds are good in salad; the ripe ones in soups, apple pie or other baked desserts. Eat the roots raw or steamed or candy them. French recipes that call for sweet cicely often call for tarragon, too. Try it in stir-fried Oriental cooking.

TARRAGON

Tarragon goes well with many things, notably fish, cheese and egg dishes, and almost any vegetable. It is an essential in *béarnaise* sauce, and was originally a must in Eggs Benedict.

In Britain you might be served tarragon consommé consisting of a heaping soupspoon of tarragon to 4 cups chicken or fish stock.

THYME

Thyme is one of the most valuable kitchen herbs. It is a traditional ingredient in clam chowder and scotch broth. Fanny Farmer, who used very few herbs, called for it in an impressive number of soups. An 1856 English cookbook calls for using it "copiously with turtles and calves heads." American pioneer cooks used thyme in corn fritters.

The early Greeks used thyme to flavor cheese and the Scandinavians still do. The Italians like it in *marinara;* the French in *bouillabaisse* and *paté de foie gras.* The Irish use thyme in Galway codling and soup, and with Limerick ham. The Hungarians use it in iced tomato soup, a summer speciality. Thyme jelly and thyme honey are delicious.

Sauté a pinch of thyme in butter to pour it over cooked vegetables.

Traditional uses of herbs

Classic Ways With Herbs— Culinary and Adventuresome

In the sections that follow, you will find ways to use herbs at their traditional best.

There are simple guides to making herb vinegars, salts, butters, wines, honey, candied flowers and teas. They are meant to give you a procedure rather than a recipe. As you experiment and taste you will discover your own recipes.

"Herbs for Fragrance," beginning on page 145, includes directions on making potpourri, sachets, lavender sticks and pomanders. Most of these are derived from recipes more than three centuries old.

"Herbs for Beauty," page 150, tells how to make shampoo, facials and face masks—just the touch needed for a day at the home beauty spa.

"Herbs for Color," page 153, is an introduction to the intricate, subtle and fine craft of making herb dyes to create your own fabric colors.

Herbs are gifts of the garden. "Herbs for Gifts" makes a fitting conclusion for this book. Begin on page 155 and read how to make some favorites—scented candles, herb-decorated stationery and herb wreaths.

An herb vinegar can be made with many kinds of herbs. Favorites include fennel, sage, rosemary, garlic and chives.

Herb Vinegars

Herbs mellow vinegar just as aging mellows wine. You can use herbs fresh or dried, but fresh herbs make better vinegars because they contain more oil than dried herbs. You can also make delicious vinegars from fresh herb seed, but you should bruise the seed first in a mortar and pestle to release flavor. You will have to strain the vinegar before final bottling.

As a general rule, use 1 cup fresh herb or 1/2 cup dried herb to flavor 1 quart of vinegar. Use cider, red wine or white wine vinegars, depending on your taste.

To avoid the possibility of chemical reaction, use glass bottles or jars with nonmetal caps. Stoppered carafes, decanters or recycled wine bottles are pretty.

Directions:

Pick branches just before flowering, or use just the leaves and tips. Wash and dry well. Fill bottles loosely with herbs. Proportion of herb-to-vinegar is a matter of taste, but remember that some herbs are stronger than others. This is especially important if you are combining two herbs in one vinegar. Cover with vinegar, cap and label. Store in a warm place for two to four weeks. Check after a few days to see that all of the herb is covered by vinegar. If not, add more. The flavor of the vinegar will strengthen the longer herbs are in the mixture. If you want a mild-flavored vinegar, strain the herbs out. If the herb flavor becomes too strong, dilute with additional vinegar. You may also want to use the herbs as needed for salads and cooking.

This ratio of fennel to vinegar pictured above is about right, but other herbs will vary in flavoring potency. Experiment and begin sampling the results a few days after it is made.

A table setting is enhanced by **flowers of blue sage, accented by a small bottle of herb vinegar.**

Herb Salts

Herb salts are a flavorful way of adding both herbs and salt to your meals. You can use either dry or fresh herbs. Salts can be made with one herb or several.

Adding paprika to herb salt gives it a nice red color and enhances the flavor.

Sprinkle herb salts on soups, stews and tomato juice, over potatoes, vegetables and casseroles.

General Rule:
1 cup of noniodized or sea salt, and 1 cup *fresh* herbs.
OR:
1 cup of noniodized or sea salt and 5 to 8 tablespoons *dry* herbs.

Herbs for herb salts: basil, chives, garlic, marjoram, oregano, rosemary, savory, tarragon and thyme.

Directions:
Crush fresh, chopped leaves with the salt, using a mortar and pestle or the base of a heavy jar, or put the salt and herbs in the blender and whirl for several minutes.

After crushing, spread the salt and herbs on a cookie sheet and dry in an oven set at 200° F (95° C) for about 40 to 60 minutes. Break up any lumps, and stir frequently during drying.

When the mixture is cool, seal in a glass jar and store it away from heat and light. Herb salts will keep indefinitely.

Using dry herbs, simply add the ingredients to a blender, whirl and bottle.

Herb salts can be made a third way, by alternately layering fresh herbs and salt in a covered jar or crock. Begin and end with slightly thicker layers of salt. This method works especially well with tarragon, basil and dill. After a few weeks, the salt will take on the flavor of the herb. Usually the herb will discolor, but any sprigs that remain green may also be used.

Ingredients and equipment needed for making herb salts.

You can shape herb butter in different ways, like these curls, balls and squares. Use a melon baller to make balls, then add texture with the paddles. The butter mold, top right, is the sort our great-great-grandparents used, and it works just as well today.

Herb Butters

The mixture of herbs with butter is a marriage made in heaven; each partner is better for the union. No one who ventures into this almost embarrassingly simple technique should require guidance on where to use herb butter. Once you have tasted it, you will want to try it not only on breads, but with vegetables, meats, fish and eggs.

Many cooks prefer to use unsalted butter, which is the French tradition. You can use fresh or dry herbs, but fresh is preferred. Don't overlook using seed.

As a general rule, use 1 tablespoon of fresh herb, 1-1/2 teaspoons dried or 1/2 teaspoon seed for each stick or 1/4 pound of butter. If you combine two or more herbs, use less of the strongly flavored ones. Some herbs become more flavorful with a few drops of lemon juice, Worcestershire sauce or vinegar, especially dried herbs. If you use one of these liquids, add them slowly and stir constantly to avoid curdling.

You can freeze and store herb butters for several weeks. Otherwise, use within a day before herbs deteriorate.

Directions:

Cream or beat room-temperature butter and stir in seasonings. Pack into molds, shape with hands into logs, or chill and form into balls, curls or pats. Refrigerate for at least three hours to allow flavors to blend.

Fines herbes butter

1 cup sweet butter
2 tablespoons parsley
2 tablespoons chives
1 tablespoon tarragon
  Try with fish, meats, poached eggs, vegetables or French bread.

Basil butter

1 cup sweet butter
1 cup fresh basil leaves, chopped (lightly packed)
4 tablespoons minced parsley (optional)
  Use with vegetables such as zucchini, eggplant, green beans; to season vegetable soups and with sautéed fish. Try frying eggs in basil butter or use on top of poached eggs.

Maitre d' Hotel butter

1 cup sweet butter
6 tablespoons finely chopped fresh parsley
2 tablespoons lemon juice
1 teaspoon Worcestershire sauce
  Excellent with broiled meats, grilled meats and fish.

Four herb butters and a loaf of homemade bread—all the ingredients for a tasting party. Left to right, the butters taste of tarragon, rosemary, chives and lemon thyme. Use fresh herb butters within a day or two. They will keep several weeks when frozen.

1/Use fresh or dried herbs finely chopped.

2/Add herbs to butter. Butter should be at room temperature.

3/Mix by hand or electric beaters.

4/Chill for 3 hours while flavors mix.

5/Enjoy with bread and other foods.

The subtle and unique flavor of May wine comes from sweet woodruff. Pansies, violets, rose petals and strawberries can be added for color.

You will discover many uses for herb honey. Combined with butter they make an excellent spread for pancakes or biscuits.

May Wine

May Day celebrations derive from ancient Druid rituals celebrating the passing of winter. We still greet May with flowers, Maypole dances and May baskets. The Germans greet her with herb-flavored May wine.

There is at least one practical reason for the herb flavoring. The wine was usually from the previous season's harvest so was less than a year old. Such wine would be thin and a bit harsh tasting. Herbs were added to improve the taste. The following is a typical May wine recipe.

Ingredients:
1 gallon dry white wine
2 tablespoons dried sweet woodruff
1/4 to 1/2 cup granulated sugar (optional)
1 bottle champagne or ginger ale
Fresh whole strawberries for decoration
Sprigs of fresh woodruff with flowers

Directions:
Pour 1 quart dry white wine into a bowl, and add the dry woodruff. Let soak overnight, stirring occasionally. Strain to remove all pieces of the woodruff. Stir in 1 bottle chilled champagne or ginger ale, 1/4 to 1/2 cup sugar (optional), and 3 quarts dry white wine.

Mix and serve with a strawberry and sprig of fresh woodruff in each glass.

Herb Honey

Herb-flavored honeys are a delightful change from standard honey. Herbs add color, fragrance, flavor and body to thin kinds of honey and fully develop the character of thicker, richer honeys.

Herb honeys are easy to make and last indefinitely. Use them to sweeten teas and punches, as a sugar substitute in salad dressings, frostings and jellies, or combine half-and-half with butter to make an excellent spread for pancakes and hot toast.

Use about 1 tablespoon fresh herb or 1 teaspoon dried herb or seed to 1 pint honey. This is no hard and fast ratio. Experiment to suit your taste.

Herbs that flavor honey: anise seeds, cardamom, cinnamon bark, coriander, fennel seeds, lavender, lemon verbena, marjoram, mints, rose geranium, rosemary, rose petals, sage, thyme and sweet violet flowers.

Directions:
Bruise fresh leaves or seeds slightly and place them in layers on the bottom of a small saucepan. Pour room-temperature honey into the pan and cook over low heat. Stir the mixture just until the honey is warm—about 2 minutes. **High heat will damage the honey.** Pour the mixture into sterilized jars and seal tightly. Store the jars at room temperature for about 1 week to allow flavors to blend. Then rewarm the honey over low heat and strain the herb leaves out. Recap or use immediately.

Candied Flowers

Candied flowers retain their color for four to six months; you can use them to decorate cakes, cookies and all kinds of desserts and fruit salads. The process requires only superfine sugar and egg white.

Borage flowers are perhaps the most colorful, but violet flowers, rose petals, mint leaves and geranium leaves can be candied in the same way. If you wish to deepen the natural flower color, use colored sugar instead of the superfine sugar called for in the directions below. Colored sugar is made by placing 1/2 cup sugar and 2 drops food coloring in a jar, and shaking until color is evenly mixed.

Pick only perfect leaves and just opened blossoms. Make sure each one has enough stem to hold onto. Wash and dry leaves, or gently shake blossoms to free them of dirt.

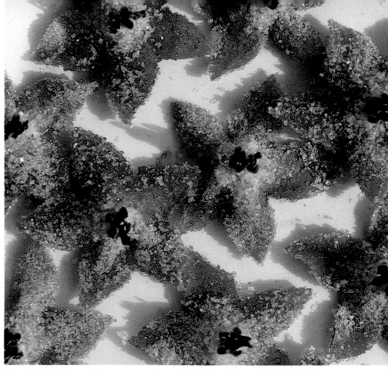

Candied borage flowers

1/Beat one egg white just until it is slightly frothy.

2/Hold the flower or leaf in one hand and paint egg white over it using a small, soft, camel's hair brush. Be sure to cover all surfaces. If necessary, use a toothpick to separate petals.

3/Sprinkle the coated leaf or flower with superfine granulated sugar. Be sure that all the petals are sugared, top and bottom. Hold petals over a bowl to save excess for reuse.

4/Place blossoms or leaves on waxed paper in a warm, dry place to dry for 2 days. Store in a tightly closed container with waxed paper between layers of flowers.

Dried forms of some favorite herb teas. Left to right: Lemon verbena, anise seed, cleveland sage, chamomile, roselle, catnip, lemongrass, lemon balm, peppermint.

Herb Teas

At one time, every house had an herb garden, and every housewife knew which herbs to use to cure a cough, fever or cold. Usually, herbs were mixed in an herbal infusion—a sweet, hot tea.

A tea brewed of catnip, chamomile and strawberry leaf was guaranteed to "calm a hysterical nature." Brewing together lemon balm, rosemary and sage created a drink known as the *immortality tea.*

The promises were big, but we shouldn't scoff. People throughout the world still use herbs as medicine. The alternatives—aspirin, penicillin, the antihistamines and vitamins—have only been used widely since the late 1920's.

Therapeutic effects aside, many herb teas taste good.

Of the many herbs that can be used for teas, most notable are mints, the lemon-flavored herbs and chamomile.

Mints—Mints are sometimes called the *candy* herbs because of their pleasing flavor. We are all accustomed to the taste of mint. It is common in a host of products from toothpaste to candy to antacids.

Mint teas are refreshing, mildly stimulating and stomach-calming. They are fine before or after dinner, and especially as a nightcap.

Use a sprig of mint, fresh or dry, to liven up a cup of English tea or to enhance a bland herb such as comfrey or alfalfa. Mints mix well.

Lemon—The flavor of lemon is not unique to the citrus fruit. Lemon balm, lemon verbena and lemongrass are all loaded with it. Mix them with a mint or chamomile for a perfect pre-bedtime tea, or with honey for a pick-up on a chilly afternoon. Lemon and mint-flavored teas are also excellent chilled summer drinks.

Chamomile—Beatrix Potter made chamomile tea familiar to many of us in her children's story, *The Tale of Peter Rabbit.* There are many kinds of chamomile, but the best chamomile tea is made with *Matricaria recutita,* German chamomile. It is an annual and its flowers have a single row of white petals.

Chamomile tea is a favorite of the Germans, and a pre-bedtime cup is said to be the only sure way to prevent nightmares.

TO MAKE HERB TEA

You will need a teapot, preferably porcelain or glass, a strainer and a timer. Warm the pot by rinsing or soaking in hot water.

Dried herbs—Use 1 teaspoon herb per cup, plus 1 for the pot. Pour in boiling water and let the mix brew for 3 minutes.

Fresh leaves—Use only a small amount until you know what you are doing. Begin with an inch-long sprig per cup, and brew for 3 or 4 minutes.

Iced tea—Brew herb tea as usual, but use about 50 percent more per portion to allow for the melting ice. Let the tea cool to room temperature, then pour over ice.

Tea herbs—Herbs that can be used in teas include: alfalfa, angelica, anise seeds, bergamot, borage, caraway seeds, German chamomile, comfrey, cumin seeds, dill seeds, elder flowers, fennel leaves or seeds, horehound, lemon balm, lemon geranium, lemongrass, lemon verbena, lovage, marigold petals, marjoram, mints, roselle, rosemary, pineapple, sage, thyme and sweet woodruff.

A WORD OF WARNING

Herb teas are an excellent substitute for coffee and ordinary tea, but some have medicinal properties that make them potentially dangerous. This is especially true if you drink them in large quantities or strong concentrations.

Here are some specific cautions to keep in mind:
• Active ingredients in herbal teas vary with the part of the plant used, the growth stage at which the plant is harvested and the growing location.
• Be absolutely sure of the identity of the plant you harvest for use in an herb tea.
• Senna pods or senna tea is a very strong laxative.
• Tea made from the peeled bark of the sassafras root contains *safrole,* a liver enzyme inhibitor suspected of increasing the risk of cancer.
• Chamomile tea can adversely affect people with ragweed allergies.
• Burdock tea becomes toxic if steeped too long.
• Alfalfa tea has a high vitamin K concentration and will counteract anticoagulant drugs.

Iced herb teas are among the most thirst-quenching summer beverages.

It is easy to make a delightful herb tea with fresh-picked leaves. First, rinse the herbs with water. Put a few sprigs in a cup or pot, then pour steaming hot water over them. Allow to steep for a few minutes, then strain.

Herbs for Fragrance

Potpourri

Although we take fragrances lightly now, originally they were not a luxury but a necessity. Before proper sanitation was understood, fresh air was considered dangerous. Castles and cottages alike needed the clean, fresh fragrance of flowers and the masking odor of herbs and spices.

It was the duty of a proper housewife to make potpourris, sweet bags and pomanders. She kept a rose jar in the best room of the house and when she finished cleaning, opened the jar and stirred the contents to allow the fragrance to permeate the room. She put sweet bags filled with rose petals and lavender in closets and linen presses, and fitted them on the backs of chairs. She strewed herbs on her floors—as did church and hospital workers—to improve room odors.

Many recipes for fragrances were concocted, and individuals were proud of their ability to compound these mixtures. For a while their most prized ingredients were found in faraway places and were extremely valued. However, it was discovered that certain common garden plants had similar odors to those of valuable spices. Some roses smelled like cinnamon, carnations like cloves. Ships brought gums, barks, beans, seed pods, even animal products, that worked as fixatives for plant fragrances. Ambergris, civet and musk are evil-smelling animal secretions that with age, proper application and blending give perfumes a rich and haunting quality. They were difficult to obtain so floral fixatives were sought and found in the root of the Florentine iris (orris root), patchouli leaves, tonka beans and vetiver roots. In 1784, lemon verbena from Mexico was brought to England, adding its cool, fresh lemon odor.

There are two kinds of potpourri, dry and moist. The original potpourris were made by the moist method. In fact the word comes from the French *pourrir* meaning to rot. But nowadays the dry method is usually used.

MATERIALS

Rose petals and buds usually compose the bulk of most potpourris. The original roses used were of the old damask type. Also very fragrant are the old-fashioned

Left: Fragrant flowers and leaves of all kinds of herbs are suitable for potpourris. But blending them to make a pleasing and long-lasting mix is the trick.

At Well-Sweep Farm in Port Murray, New Jersey, harvested flowers are cleaned, sorted, arranged and readied for drying.

Bundles of flowers are tied with string to poles that are set across barn rafters. See photo page 5.

cabbage rose and the Kanzanlik, which has been grown for centuries for *attar* or *otto* of roses, the essential oil distilled from rose blossoms. Gallica roses retain flower color when dry as does the modern rose 'Dainty Bess'.

Many other flowers can be used in addition to or instead of the roses. Some of the others have little or no scent, but this can be remedied by the addition of essential oils and proper fixatives. To test whether a flower would be useful, pick one and hang it in a dry place for a few days. Check to see if it retains its color. Even if it doesn't, it can be used for bulk. The fragrant plants that are listed here can be grown in any garden that has some sun and a well-drained soil.

Brandy, called for in many recipes, is used to revive tired sachets and potpourris, because the alcohol releases the latent scent molecules in the dry materials. For centuries the ancients had no notion of alcohol's ability to dissolve and release aromatics. Wine was the first solvent; now brandy is used, a few drops for an old sachet, a tablespoon for a weak potpourri.

Orris root is one of the most commonly used fixatives to hold the fragrance of the ingredients in potpourri. The root is washed until free of soil, peeled, chopped and dried.

Fragrant Leaves: Bay, lavender, lemon balm, lemon geranium, lemon thyme, lemon verbena, thyme, mint, oregano, patchouli, geranium, rosemary, sweet basil, sweet marjoram, sweet woodruff and tarragon.

Fragrant Flowers and Petals: Lavender, pinks, roses, chamomile.

Colorful petals and flowers: Blue: Borage, cornflower, delphinium, lavender and violets; **Yellow:** Broom, chamomile, calendula, primrose, tansy and yarrow; **Red or pink:** Monardas, hibiscus, hollyhock and roses.

Spices: Allspice, calamus root, cinnamon bark or sticks, cloves, frankincense, myrrh, sandalwood, vetiver root.

Fragrant Seeds: Anise, coriander.

Fixatives: Fixatives are used to hold the fragrance of the ingredients. They absorb the vital oils and retard evaporation. They come powdered or ground; either will do, but the powder clouds glass containers. As a general rule, use 1 tablespoon or 1/2 ounce fixative for every quart of petals. Fixatives easiest to find are orris root, vetiver and citrus peels. Gum benzoin and tonka bean are good fixatives that are available from herb-craft suppliers.

Essential Oils: These are volatile oils that evaporate at room temperature and spread the potpourri fragrance. Do not use the extracts on the spice shelves in grocery stores, and don't add too many different kinds of oils as they tend to counteract one another. The most common essential oils are oil of violet, carnation, jasmine, lemon verbena, lavender, sandalwood, heliotrope and orange blossom (or *neroli*). Attar of roses is the most desirable of all the oils.

COLLECTING THE INGREDIENTS

Gather the flowers as soon as they open and continue adding to the collection through the blooming season. Gather them on a warm, sunny day as soon as the dew has dried. Select blooms that have recently opened, not old ones ready to drop their petals. To dry, remove petals from the flowers and spread them out thinly on newspaper or a screen. Place them in a warm, dry, shady spot where they will dry quickly and without appreciable loss of their fragrance. Dry whole flowers by spreading a 1/2-inch layer of borax, fine sand, or silica gel in the bottom of a box. Place the whole flower on the sand. Cover completely with more sand. Keep the box in a warm, dry place until the flowers are dry. More information about drying herbs is found on page 120.

DRY POTPOURRI

Let the petals, herbs and leaves dry until they are crisp. Mix them thoroughly in a large bowl and blend in the other spices, adding them a little at a time until the desired fragrance is obtained. Add essential oils to the fixative and add the fixative to the other ingredients last. After you have blended all ingredients, store for a month to ripen in a dark, closed container, shaking occasionally, then transfer them to pretty jars for gifts.

A small potpourri requires about 2 ounces of dry mixture, and a large one—enough to fill a large crock—requires about 3 pounds. Most people prefer the dry method for making potpourris, but any recipe can be used with either method. Do remember that the initial aroma is much different than the finished mature odor. Have patience and avoid the temptation of using too much oil.

DRY POTPOURRI RECIPES

Rose-lavender potpourri—Start with 10 ounces each rose petals and lavender blossoms. Add 5 ounces sweet rose leaves and 2 ounces ground orris root. Combine with 3/4 ounce crushed cinnamon bark, 1/2 ounce each allspice and cloves. Then add 6 drops of tonka bean oil or 10 ground tonka beans. Mix well and let season for one month.

Bay-rose potpourri—This calls for a large quantity of rose petals. If you don't have this amount, reduce accordingly. The general rule is to mix 1 tablespoon fixative to 1 quart rose petals and add 1 tablespoon spice. Take 3 quarts rose petals and add 12 torn bay leaves, 2 handfuls lavender flowers and 1 handful each

For an extra special potpourri, add these ingredients to basic potpourri recipes: Clockwise from top is dried citrus peel, coriander seeds, grated nutmeg, orris root, anise seeds, allspice, cinnamon sticks and cloves. All are ground coarse with the mortar and pestle or grinder, and mixed together. Essential oils are added before the mix is incorporated with other potpourri ingredients.

orange blossoms, violets and clove carnations. Mix in 2 ounces orris root, 1 ounce ground nutmeg, 1/4 ounce each cinnamon and ground clove. Sprinkle mix with 1/2 ounce oil of neroli. Mix and season for one month.

Spice potpourri—Mix 1 quart rose petals with 1/2 pint lavender flowers, 1 teaspoon anise seed and 1 tablespoon each of cloves, nutmeg and cinnamon mixed together and crushed, 1 tablespoon crushed benzoin, and 5 drops each oil of jasmine, rose geranium, patchouli and rosemary. Mix well and let season for one month.

Lavenderwood potpourri—This has an old-fashioned, delicate fragrance. Combine 16 ounces lavender flowers with 2 ounces sweet woodruff, 1-1/2 ounces each moss and thyme, 8 ounces slivered orange peel, 4 ounces benzoin and several handfuls of other flowers such as cornflowers or violets. Finish off with 1/4 ounce clove and anise combined. Mix and let season. This mix is particularly nice for sachets.

MOIST POTPOURRI

The moist method has several advantages. You do not have to be as careful when handling the materials as you do with the dry method, and the scent has greater staying power. Some moist potpourris have retained their perfumes for as long as 50 years. The scent of moist potpourri is usually a bit heavier than dry potpourri regardless of the ingredients used. Wet potpourri is kept in a covered, nontransparent jar. When the aroma is desired, the cover is removed for a period of time, then replaced.

To make moist potpourri, use the flowers and leaves when they are soft and leathery, not crisp—just very limp with about one-third of their bulk gone. Place in a large, wide-mouthed glass or ceramic container with a tight cover; use a long wooden spoon for mixing. Let this mixture set for 1 week and then stir as it matures. It matures in the container for at least 2 weeks. Add a layer of the material and cover it with a layer of common, noniodized, salt. Continue to alternate layers of petals and salt until the container is about three-fourth full or you have exhausted your supply of petals. You can add more flowers throughout the summer, but each batch needs at least 2 weeks to mature. Use a plate with a rock on it to press on the mass.

Make sure your container is large enough to handle the quantity of materials in the recipes below. If necessary, you can proportion the recipe to a half or quarter.

Potpourris have many uses. Open covered jars to release a roomful of fragrance or stir in an open bowl. Sachets—potpourri filled—can be simple or fancy. Attach to a hanger and the fragrance will permeate clothing. Sachets will remain scented for many years if kept in dresser drawers.

MOIST POTPOURRI RECIPES

Brown sugar potpourri—You will need 2 gallons of partially dried rose petals. Lay them in 1/2-inch layers in a container, alternating with 1/2-inch layers of coarse salt. You can make a special bay salt by taking 1 pound noniodized salt and crushing 6 bay leaves into it with a mortar and pestle. Estimate the quantity of salt you will use and make up an equal quantity of a mixture of allspice, cloves and brown sugar, 1/4 pound gum benzoin and 2 ounces crushed orris root. This goes in with the salt layers. Add 1/4 pint brandy and any sort of fragrant flowers you have on hand. Citrus leaves, lemon verbena and rose geranium leaves can also be added. Allow this mixture to age for a month, stirring thoroughly every day. This is an old recipe and

is said to retain its perfume for at least 50 years with the occasional addition of some brandy.

Orange-mint potpourri—You will need 8 ounces of fresh or partially wilted orange blossoms. Mix these with 4 ounces mint leaves, 3 ounces well-crushed coriander seeds, 1 ounce each benzoin and oakmoss, 2 ounces each of ground vetiver and calamus root. Store in a container by alternating this mixture with layers of salt that has been ground with rosemary.

Violet potpourri—To an ounce of ground orris root add 4 ounces dried rose leaves, 2 ounces benzoin, 2 ounces ground tonka bean, 4 ounces mint leaves, 1/8 ounce bitter almond and 1/4 ounce violet oil. You can add violet flowers for color, but they contribute no fragrance. Mix and alternate with salt in a container.

Lavender Sticks

Lavender sticks add the penetrating scent of lavender to your closets and drawers. They are not difficult to make and the fragrance is lasting. Each stick will require approximately 4 feet of 1/4-inch satin ribbon.

Directions:

Gather fresh lavender flower spikes that have long stems. The lower flowers along the spike should be fully opened and the higher ones just beginning to open. Strip off the lowest leaves.

Gather an uneven number of stems together; 13, 15 or 17 is about the right number. Tie them tightly with string just below their lowest flowers.

Bend the green and pliable stems back over the flower buds, as shown in the photo.

Tuck the end of the ribbon into the buds and begin to weave over one stem and under the next. Continue weaving around the buds until they are enclosed. Work carefully to prevent stems from breaking. Wrap remaining ribbon around stems. Cover the loose ends with a small satin bow, and place wherever you want the aroma of lavender.

To make lavender sticks, bend stems back over flower buds. Tuck one end of the ribbon into the buds and weave.

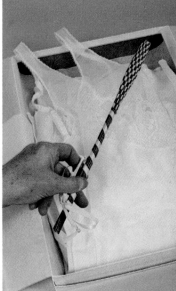

Wrap remaining ribbon around stems. Use to perfume satins, silks and other delicate linens.

Pomanders

The first pomanders were hollow balls filled with various herbs and spices. As elaborate as jewelry, they were made of gold, silver, ivory or china and were worn around the neck or waist to cover foul odors and for their supposed antiseptic properties. Today a pomander is a citrus fruit, studded with cloves and dried, made for hanging in a closet to perfume clothes and repel moths. They are also nice as a Christmas tree decoration, or mounded in a bowl with greenery.

Pomanders are fun to make and give, but they do require time and patience.

Directions:

Start with *firm*, unblemished, ripe oranges and an ample supply of unbroken whole cloves.

Make a hole in the orange skin with a toothpick and insert a clove. Cover the entire surface of the orange with closely set cloves. It will take approximately 1 hour for each pomander.

You can roll the pomander in a mixture of spices and orris root to add more aroma. Mix powdered cinnamon, allspice, nutmeg, coriander and orris root according to preference, but any of these ingredients can be omitted.

Allow the pomander to dry at room temperature for several weeks. When dry it will shrink and harden.

When thoroughly dry, tie securely with ribbon and bow, or wrap in a square of tulle or net.

Pomanders are pungently fragrant and easy to make, though time consuming.

A few of the herbal cosmetics you can make include soaps, rubbing lotions, shampoos, hair tonics and rinses.

Herbs for Beauty

Cosmetics

Herbal cosmetics and bath and skin care preparations are easy to make, economical and contain no harmful additives or preservatives. Making your own shampoo, perfume and herbal lotions with common garden herbs might seem farfetched at first, but try a couple and see if you don't get hooked on them.

Do be aware that without the preservatives of commercial products, herbal cosmetics are not long lasting. The exceptions are alcohol or vinegar-based preparations. Whenever you use fresh plants, make small amounts and use as soon as possible. You can't store herb preparations too long, but keeping them in the refrigerator will slow deterioration.

There is a nearly infinite variety of recipes for herbal cosmetics, each of which can be varied to some degree to suit your own tastes. On these pages are some of the very best.

HAIR CARE

Easy-to-Make Herb Shampoo

Make a good herb shampoo by pouring 1 cup boiling water over 2 teaspoons of dried herb or 2 tablespoons fresh herb. Steep overnight, then strain and add the liquid to a purchased shampoo. Mild baby shampoo is a favorite.

Old Herbal Hair Tonic

1/4 cup dried rosemary leaves
1/8 cup dried sage leaves
1 tablespoon dried nettle leaves
2 cups alcohol
1/8 cup olive oil
1/8 cup castor oil

Directions:

Grind or chop the dried herbs, then soak them in alcohol for 7 to 10 days. Strain out the herbs and add the oils. Add just enough distilled water to produce a slightly milky look, then bottle.

SKIN CARE

Herb Facials

Beneficial to all types of skin, this herbal steam—popular in expensive spas for the deep cleaning of pores—costs very little to do at home.

Steam method:

Bring 4 tablespoons dried chamomile flowers and 2 cups distilled water to a boil and remove pot from heat. Cover your hair with a towel. Drape another large towel over your head and the pot. Keep your face at least a foot away from the steaming pot. Steam face for 5 to 10 minutes. Lift towel to get fresh air if needed during facial. Wash with an astringent lotion to close pores.

Compress method:

Make the chamomile mix as described in the steam method. Drape a towel over your shoulders to catch any drips. Dip a clean wash cloth into the hot tea. Carefully lift cloth out with tongs and press against the side of the pot. Apply to your face while reasonably hot. Repeat until the tea cools. Especially good for the back of the neck.

Face Mask for All Types of Skin

1 fresh egg white
1 tablespoon dry milk
1 teaspoon honey
1/4 teaspoon finely chopped fresh chamomile flowers, fennel, parsley, lemongrass or mint leaves

Directions:

Combine ingredients in a bowl using a whisk, or place in a blender at low speed for 2 minutes or until creamy. Apply cream to face and throat; let it remain on skin for 15 minutes. As the cream dries, it will form a mask. Remove the mask with warm water; then splash face with cold water.

Honey Mask for Dry Skin

1 teaspoon honey
1 teaspoon finely ground fennel seed
1 teaspoon olive oil
1 egg yolk

Directions:

Combine the ingredients in a small bowl and mix well. Cover face and throat with mixture, allowing it to remain on skin for 30 minutes. Remove with lukewarm water.

HERB BATHS

Tie 1 cup or more of your favorite dried herbs or 2 to 3 cups fresh herbs into a loose bag of cheesecloth or nylon hose. This makes them easy to discard. Put the bag into an enamel pan and cover with water. Bring to a boil and turn off heat. Cover with a lid, so the fragrant steam won't escape, and steep for 15 minutes. Pour into a tub of warm water and enjoy!

Suggested bath herbs:

bay leaves	marjoram leaves
chamomile flowers	mint leaves
lavender flowers	thyme leaves
lemon balm leaves	rose petals
lemongrass	

Follow with a fragrant dusting powder or after-bath lotion.

Herbs For Color

Natural Dyes

The fact that man can make his own colors from plant material was likely discovered accidentally—when berries stained fingers, or a bed of crushed leaves discolored clothing. That happened about 3,000 years ago, but excitement over natural dyes still runs high among spinners, weavers, basketmakers, potters, tie-dyers, batik artists and crafts people. They talk with pride about the subtle, custom colors they get and the control they retain. They talk with joy about understanding "the intimate relationship between man and his environment."

At first it was a matter of random experiment, but finding and using dye plants effectively evolved fairly rapidly. Each part of the world developed color schemes characteristic of its region. The beautiful Tyrian purple, or royal purple, of the Mediterranean countries came from the sea snail, murex; the famous bayeta red of Navajo blankets—and probably the red Betsy Ross used for the United States flag—came from cochineal, the small insects that infest some species of *Opuntia* cacti. There are only a few animal sources of dye, and cochineal is the only one still used commercially. The plants of dim, foggy Scotland produced all the bright myriad colors for tartans except blue; for it they imported indigo, from certain plants of the genus *Indigofera*.

By the 1800's the great dye houses of Europe considered dye making a science, and the production of multicolored yarns and cloth was big business.

Only a dozen or so plants were used commercially: those that have great concentrations of color pigment, with the quality of fastness. But there were hundreds of indigenous plants available to householders. A Frenchman of the 18th century, looking for good dye plants in the New World, found more than 500 plants in the New England countryside.

COLOR TALK

Most people who use natural dyes talk about the earthy, gentle tones that plants provide, but reports to the contrary notwithstanding, natural dyes can be extremely bright. But all have a unique quality that is difficult to describe. They are never harsh or garish, and they never clash with each other. Perhaps the best way to describe them is to say that they have a natural brightness, like a flower.

Newcomers to the art are likely to claim that natural dyes don't fade. Not true. They do fade, some very

Left: Skeins of naturally dyed wool and the materials used in the dying process.

quickly, some in a hundred years or so . . . but they fade "true." Blue stays blue, but it gets softer. The same goes for all the other colors. It might well be true that some natural dyes would outlast their fabrics if that were possible. Coptic textiles of the 5th and 6th centuries still retain faint, mellow reds, blues, greens and browns, after 1,500 years, and pre-Columbian Peruvian fabrics remain rich and vibrant with golds, a pinkish red and a green that is almost black. The fabrics themselves—soft and usually short-lived—have survived only because they were underground or in caves.

Natural dyeing takes you into many fascinating studies, including the fields of botany, chemistry and art. The plants alone offer a wide range of colors; when you learn what alteration in colors are possible, you can develop shades, hues and tints just as painter mixes his colors on a palette.

In the 1st century Dioscorides and Pliny the Elder recorded that they used madder for red; indigo for blue; saffron and weld for yellow; oak bark, walnuts, and gall for brown.

Here are some color plants to look for or plant today.

Red—Madder root, which gives old Oriental rugs their deep turkey reds, produces the best and most lasting red tones. Of the same family as lady's bedstraw, the leaves are sandpaper-rough on their lower surface. Tiny yellow flowers appear in spring in clusters above the leaves.

After three year's growth, the roots are dug, cleaned, dried and ground. Soak about 8 ounces of powdered root overnight, then boil and immediately strain through gauze for dye water.

Use alum as a mordant to fix the brightest reds. Use chrome for a garnet red.

Yellow—You will have to get yellow from flowers, and flowers do not usually produce good dyes unless they are yellow. Some are not as colorfast as others. Weld, probably the most colorfast of all plant dyes, will last several thousands of years, but narcissus might give out in a year or two, depending on the amount of sunlight and washing it must take.

There are many sources of yellow. Some of the best are lady's bedstraw, saffron, safflower, agrimony, weld and St. John's wort.

Blue—Because few plants produce blue, indigo has been a valuable, expensive article of trade since the beginning of sailing ships and traders. It was well known in the ancient world for the clarity and fastness of blue it produced. Native to the East Indies, its use spread rapidly throughout the world.

Indigo dye is made by fermenting plant leaves. Branches are immersed in water until they ferment. The residue that settles to the vat bottom is formed into cakes. Very few craftsmen process their own dye from the plant today; indigo powder, ready to use, is available from craft supply shops.

Woad, which the Druids used to color their bodies, is native to the British Isles. It is a tall, yellow-flowered relative of mustard and contains the same dye chemicals as indigo, but in less concentrated form.

Grays, blacks, browns and greens and the infinite number of shades and tints of each are also obtainable from plants. Once you get interested you'll want to begin experimenting with all kinds of other plants including trees, shrubs and weeds.

MORDANTS

There are two processes involved in dyeing: mordanting and dyeing. The lasting quality of colors depends on mordanting, so this process is just as important as dyeing itself.

The word *mordant* is derived from the Latin word *mordere,* meaning *to bite.* Mordants are used to chemically combine with the dye and "fix" it to the material.

A few plant dyes, such as the browns from walnuts and some tree barks, do not require a mordant, but most require one for permanent color.

You can dye a wide range of shades in one dye pot if you premordant your yarn with four or five different minerals; by having some already dyed with one color; or by using gray or brown yarns. And you can tie some areas to resist the mordant and therefore the dye. You can mordant before, during or after dyeing. It is the principle involved, not the exact formula or recipe.

Common mordants are alum and cream of tartar, tartaric acid. Other mordants for special effects are:

Chrome, potassium dichromate, is used for deepening yellow and gold tones. Always keep a lid on the pot as it is light sensitive. It is also poisonous, so keep it away from pets and children. Use 1/2 ounce to 4 gallons water.

Copper, cupric sulfate, turns greenish yellows to good greens. Dyeing in a copper pot will do the same thing. Use 1/4 ounce to 4 gallons water.

Iron, ferrous sulfate, darkens most colors. The colonials called this "saddening." Use 1/4 ounce plus 1 ounce cream of tartar to 4 gallons water.

Tin, stannous chloride, brightens colors, called "blooming." Use 1/4 ounce plus 1 ounce cream of tartar to 4 gallons water.

When you add chrome, copper, iron or tin to the dye bath itself do so about 15 minutes before the end of dyeing time. Remove the yarn, add minerals and dissolve thoroughly, then replace yarn or other material.

To alter colors, dip the material immediately into either an acid, vinegar or alkaline (ammonia) afterbath for about 15 minutes.

A BASIC RECIPE

The standard mordant for any and all natural dyes is a combination of alum and cream of tartar. For 1 pound of fleece, yarn or any wool, use 3 ounces alum and 1 ounce cream of tartar in 4 gallons of water. Include about 1 tablespoon washing soda or other water softener if your water is hard. For more or less yarn, simply proportion these ingredients. Use other mordants for special effects.

Other materials can be dyed, but wool in any of its forms is by far the easiest. Synthetic materials are not easily colored by natural dyes.

Add previously wetted wool and slowly bring to boil; reduce heat and simmer for 1 hour. Your mordanting is now complete and you can dye immediately or dry and dye at a later time. If it is to be used later be sure to tag it "alum mordanted" and date.

American dyers prefer enamel pots. They do not react at all with the dye or mordant. In New Zealand, aluminum pots are preferred for their brightening effect. Copper pots add a green tint and iron pots darken colors.

If you have two large pots you can brew your dye at the same time you mordant. First, take lots of plant material—an armful of leaves and branches; a shopping bag full of any kind of yellow flower; a plastic vegetable bag full of onion skins. Your market produce man will be your best source for onion skins.

If you have a heavy or woody dye material soak it overnight. Other materials can be used as soon as picked, or dried and used later.

Boil plant material in soft water until a good color is obtained. It may take one hour or several. Strain and add mordanted wool. Simmer 1 hour, or longer, rinse and dry in the shade. If the dye bath still has good color, add more yarn to get a lighter shade, and again for a still lighter one.

Many plants that lose their color when boiled can be fermented instead. One of the best is the prickly pear, the fruit of the opuntia cactus. Mash fruit, add small amount of water and let stand in warm place a week or two, preferably downwind. Strain and add just enough water to give you enough dye bath to work with. Add yarn or what you wish to dye, and let sit for a week or two. Check it occasionally, work the dye through the material with your hands. Remove when the color is what you like.

HAVE FUN

Much of the pleasure of natural dyeing comes from approaching it easily and calmly. Don't demand exactly the color you have in mind; instead, appreciate the colors that plants produce.

An arrangement of homemade, herb-scented candles.

Herbs For Gifts

Fragrant candles are fun to make, and their sweet scent is a pleasant reminder of summer's garden.

Use either paraffin or beeswax. Both will take a color and fragrance, but beeswax is generally considered to have superior burning qualities. They may also be mixed in any desired proportion.

Fragrant herbs to experiment with include rosemary, rose petals, lemon verbena, lavender flowers, lemon or orange peel. They should be finely chopped if fresh, or powdered if dried.

Wax and other materials are available in most markets or craft supply shops.

Materials:
2 pounds wax, broken into chunks
2 cups dried herbs, or 3 cups fresh herbs
2 crayons or sticks of candle colorant shaved into small chips
2—11 inch candle wicks
2 candle molds, 8 x 3 inches

NOTE: Be careful when melting wax because it is highly flammable. Melt it in a double boiler—never directly over heat—and don't leave unattended.

Spread newspaper over the working surface to make cleanup of spilled wax easy.

When thoroughly melted, remove from heat and stir in coloring. Let the wax cool slightly before adding herb fragrance. If the wax begins to set, it may be reheated.

Prepare the mold by lightly coating the insides with silicone spray or petroleum jelly. Wrap one end of the wick around a pencil or stick allowing enough to extend the depth of the mold. Center the wick over the mold as shown in the photo below.

As wax cools, mix in herbs. Stir occasionally to make sure herbs are distributed throughout wax.

When wax has a consistency of almost-set jello, pour into mold. After about 45 minutes use a pencil to make a small hole in crust near wick. Fill this hole with hot wax. Otherwise a well forms around the wick as the wax hardens and shrinks. Allow to set. When cool, remove carefully from the mold. Trim edges of the candle with knife and polish with an old nylon stocking.

Here are all the tools and ingredients you need to make herb candles. Add scent with fresh herb or herb oil.

Pressed flowers and leaves are easy to make—all you really need is a heavy book. Once dried, use them to decorate greeting cards or stationery, or frame them.

Decorating Stationery and Cards with Herbs

Collecting flowers and leaves of herbs for pressing is a simple and pleasant way to spend an afternoon. All you need is an old telephone book and some small scissors. As you admire your plants, tuck the occasional perfect specimen into the book.

Store plants when thoroughly dry for about three weeks inside a phone book between pieces of waxed paper, blotting paper or construction paper until ready to use.

Position herbs on cards or stationery with tweezers. To make a pleasing arrangement, vary the sizes and shapes for contrast. Use a small amount of white glue or rubber cement to attach the herbs. Push the glue or rubber cement underneath the leaves, stems or petals while you hold them in place. Press until dry.

Protect arrangements on cards with clear, self-adhesive vinyl contact paper.

Herb Wreaths

Wreaths derive from the ancient and nearly universal reverence of the circle as a symbol of eternity. The use of decorative greenery during the winter comes from the Druids, and the idea of shaping greenery to make rings has distant origins in Hellenic and Hebrew custom. By the time of St. Augustine, about 700 A.D., all of these elements combined into Christian custom.

Plants for wreaths at one time had specific meanings. The Druids favored holly because witches feared it; later it came to symbolize Christ's crown of thorns. Bay laurel symbolized the triumph of humanity; yew and cypress, eternal life. Juniper at one time meant sanctuary, and fir, patience. Warriors fought for a crown of oak leaves; poets won a garland of ivy. Mistletoe was placed over the door as a symbol of peace and friendship. Many other plants have been used to make wreaths, among them grasses, ivy, myrtle, euonymus, mosses and ferns.

Herbs make nice wreaths because they will dry in place and remain fragrant for weeks. Favorite herbs for wreaths are germander, gray or green santolina, sweet lavender, myrtle, thyme, rosemary, rue, oregano, tansy and yarrow.

You can use almost any ring as a frame for an herb wreath. It is possible to buy rings of styrofoam into which sprigs of dried herbs are easily inserted. A wire frame filled with *damp* sphagnum moss can be used for *fresh* sprigs of herbs. Manufactured wire wreaths are available from some florist and craft shops, or you can make your own wire frame. Roll a piece of chicken wire into a tube, then bend it until the two ends meet to form a circle. Tie the ends together with wire and cover it with fresh herbs.

Wreaths are versatile. When not hanging, they make attractive centerpieces or decorative bases for candles, serving dishes or punch bowls.

Tools and materials:

Styrofoam, wire or chicken wire frame
Florist's wire, 24-gauge
Wire cutters
Pliers
Kitchen shears
Hand pruner
Gloves
Leaves and branches of herbs for the kind of wreath you plan
Ribbon for a bow (optional)

Wreaths are among the most dramatic of the many herbal gifts you can prepare.

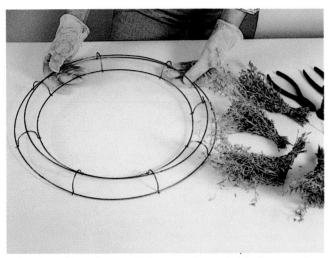

1/Begin with a frame. This type is available from craft or florist's shops.

2/Attach herb bunches to the wire frame with 24-gauge florist's wire.

3/Continue layering the herb bunches until you reach the desired thickness and density.

4/Once the foundation layer is complete, fill in with dried flowers or other herb bunches of a complementary color.

Glossary

Annual—A plant that completes its life cycle in one season.

Apothecary—A person who makes, sells and prescribes herbal medicines.

Aromatic—Materials of pungent, spicy scent and pleasing taste. Mildly stimulating fragrances. Many aromatic herbs were thought to heal or prevent disease.

Astringent—Any material that causes the skin to contract.

Balm—A soothing ointment obtained from a variety of herbs and trees. Derives from the word *balsam.* Applied to several mint family plants such as *Mellisa officinalis,* lemon balm, and *Monarda didyma,* bee balm.

Biennial—A plant that completes its life cycle in 2 growing seasons, usually flowering and fruiting the second year.

Blender—A perfumer's term referring to a secondary, complementary fragrance in a perfume blend.

Botany—The science of studying plants, including their growth, form, function and classification.

Bruise—To lightly pound herb stems and leaves.

Calyx—All of the sepals, considered collectively as one unit.

Deciduous—Term applied to plant that loses leaves or other parts during its dormant season of the year. Plant seems to die, but returns to life in the spring.

Decoction—An herbal preparation made by boiling an herb, usually a seed, root or bark, in a covered container for 15 minutes. The liquid is strained and the herb residue discarded.

Dioscorides—Greek physician considered the father of modern botany. Author of *Materia medica,* published in 60 A.D., most authoritative herbal for more than 1,500 years.

Distill—The process of extracting an herbal essence by boiling the herb in a liquid and condensing the rising vapor.

Elixir—A distillation of tincture.

Essence—A solution of 1 ounce essential oil in 1 pint of alcohol.

Essential oil—Volatile and fragrant oils produced in the various parts of many herbs. They are used to bring out the full aroma of potpourri mixtures. Available from herbcraft suppliers.

Evergreen—Plants that have green leaves throughout the year.

Extract—A strong decoction.

Fixative—A perfumer's term that refers to substances added to a perfume or potpourri blend to absorb and preserve the delicate fragrances.

Floret—One small, individual flower in a cluster of flowers.

Genus—The most important subdivision of a plant or animal family. The first word of a two-word Latin name. *Ocimum* is the genus of basil.

Herb—Plant whose leaves, stems or roots are used for food, medicine, flavor or fragrance. Nonwoody or semi-woody plant; the stem remains more or less succulent. Most herbs are easily cultivated in the home garden.

Herb Society of America—Founded in 1933 and dedicated to the use and delight of herbs. Members receive *Herbarist* and *Report On Annual Meeting* once a year, and a quarterly newsletter. For membership information, write: Central Office for Information and Publication, Herb Society of America, Horticultural Hall, 300 Massachusetts Avenue, Boston, MA 02115.

Herbal—A book of herb information and legend.

Herbalism—The study of herbs.

Herbalist—Individual skilled in the indentification and use of herbs. Originally a description of a botanist and author of an herbal.

Herbarium—A collection of dried plants made for the purpose of botanical study.

Herb oils—Made by bruising herb leaves and stems and covering them with a light vegetable oil in a covered jar.

Hippocrates—Greek physician and herbalist considered the father of modern medicine.

Homeopathy—A system of medical treatment based on the theory that some diseases are cured by an herb that will produce the symptoms of that disease in healthy people.

Infusion—An herbal drink made by pouring boiling water on fresh or dried herbs, allowing them to steep a few minutes, then straining out the herb residue. Most herb teas are infusions.

Knot garden—English term for a garden design based on patterns used by weavers and lace makers. Popular from 16th century to late 18th century. They were made on level ground, usually in front of a house, with plants such as germander, dwarf lavenders, common thyme and lavender cotton.

Macerate—Soaking in water or alcohol to soften.

Mordant—Substance used in dyeing to fix the coloring matter to the object.

Mortar and pestle—A hard bowl and club-like tool with which to pound and grind seeds and other materials.

Mulch—A layer of material such as straw, bark or plastic laid over the soil. A mulch will slow water evaporation and prevent soil heaving due to alternate freezing and thawing.

Perennial—A plant that lives for more than 2 years, though it may die to the ground or become dormant during adverse seasons.

Pliny The Elder—Roman naturalist and author of *Naturalis Historia,* a voluminous compilation of all known facts about nature, including chapters on trees, plants and medicinal herbs. Published approximately 50 A.D.

Posset—A hot, spiced drink of milk curdled by ale or wine.

Potion—An herbal drink.

Potpourri—French term translating literally as *rotten pot.* A mixture of fragrant flowers, herbs and spices.

Rhizome—A thick, fleshy underground stem that can develop both roots and leafy shoots.

Sachet—A small bag filled with herbs and spices used to scent clothing.

Sepals—Individual segments of the calyx that surrounds the petals.

Simple—A medicinal plant or herb.

Solution—The liquid mixture of water or alcohol and another thoroughly dissolved substance.

Spice—A strongly flavored, aromatic substance usually obtained from tropical plants. With a few exceptions, spices are not readily grown in home gardens.

Sprig—A small, 2 or 3-inch twig cut from the tips of an herb.

Stillroom—The special room 17th century housewives used to prepare a variety of household necessities from her own garden herbs.

Strewing herbs—During medieval times, fragrant herbs strewn on the floor to freshen the room's air.

Tincture—A mixture of an herb extract in alcohol, usually for medicinal purposes. Very dilute medicinal substance in alcohol.

Tisane—French word for an herb tea.

Umbel—A flat-topped flower cluster typical of parsley and its relatives.

Variegated—Used to describe leaves with different colors, usually in streaks or spots.

Volatile—A quickly evaporating material.

Wort—Anglo-Saxon word originally meaning *root,* eventually used to mean just about any kind of plant; synonymous with *herb.* By the middle of the 17th century, the word *plant* replaced wort, except in the names of some old plants for which it had become a suffix, such as mugwort.